molić WY

WITHDRAWN

WORLDS APART

WORLDS APART

A MUSLIM GIRL WITH THE SAS

AZI AHMED

The Robson Press

First published in Great Britain in 2015 by
The Robson Press (an imprint of Biteback Publishing Ltd)
Westminster Tower
3 Albert Embankment
London SE1 7SP
Copyright © Azi Ahmed 2015

ISBN 978-1-84954-779-6

10 9 8 7 6 5 4 3 2 1

A CIP catalogue record for this book is available from the British Library.

Set in Stempel Garamond

Printed and bound in Great Britain by
CPI Group (UK) Ltd, Croydon CR0 4YY

MIX
Paper from
responsible sources
FSC® C020471

*I would like to dedicate this book
to my parents and sister*

CONTENTS

This book is based on the experiences and recollections of the author. In some cases, people, places, procedures and dates have been changed to protect the privacy and security of others.

PROLOGUE

'OH YES, MY daughter's a very good cook.' Mum smiled at the three guests sat on the floral sofa.

I pulled the headscarf tight around my head and hobbled over to serve them chai. I knelt down at the coffee table. My knees were swollen to the size of grapefruits underneath my shalwar. The bruises on my arms were hidden by a long-sleeved kameez and my blistered feet were bandaged and covered up with socks. So far, my parents were none the wiser about these marks and bruises, and I wanted to keep it that way.

People coming over to eye me up didn't worry me as much as it used to. I had a very clear view of what I didn't want, but for some reason I still went along with it. I kept telling myself, *be normal, be normal, be normal*; Mum has a sixth sense.

One of the guests, a man called Majid, reached for a samosa from the plate I'd put down in front of him. He looked about fifty, dark, had a pot-holed complexion with a mop of black oily hair. My eyes slid across to his wife who wore large tinted glasses and a white shawl wrapped around her head and shoulders. The combination of her strong musky perfume and Mum's air freshener almost knocked me out.

Their son was nestled between them, looking too scared to move. He was a younger-looking version of his father with a potbelly and goggly eyes.

'I'm sure your daughter is a very good cook.' Majid spoke to my mum as if I was invisible. 'But will she cook for Rajas?'

Mum suddenly sat up straight in the armchair. Rajas were one of the highest castes in Pakistan, something villagers like us don't get close to under normal circumstances. But this wasn't normal; this was England. She traced her aubergine lips with an Aztec gold fingernail before answering. 'Rest assured, brother, my daughter is not the modern type. She attends mosque every day, prays five times, doesn't go out alone...'

It is amazing the lengths parents go to make their children sparkle in front of others.

I glanced at my dad, who was sitting by the bay window, gazing out at the traffic. As always, he was dressed in his dapper way; crisp beige shirt, hand-knitted cream pullover and Jesus sandals with thick white sports socks. I admired his tolerance; nothing ever got to him and he completely ignored people that talked too much, including Mum. He was my tower of strength.

Majid suddenly roared with laughter at something Mum had said. Mum joined in. Her giggles escalated into squeals, making her sparkly headscarf slip down to expose her frizzy black hair, tied back in a peach pearl bobble.

Majid reached out to Dad, offering him a low five, who in return stared at the hand glistening in oil and bits of pastry from the samosa. He smacked it politely, making Majid roar even louder and elbow his son.

The room became quiet again. Majid began picking the food from between his teeth with a fingernail. I could tell Mum was racking her brains for something to say. She didn't like gaps in conversation.

'What did your daughter study at college?' Majid asked.

'Art,' Mum said.

'Art? What's that?'

'It's a degree.'

Shaking his head, Majid reached into his pocket and

brought out a packet of cigarettes. 'If I had a daughter, I would never let her leave home to study. This country is very bad for our girls.'

'That depends how much you trust your children,' Mum retorted, struggling out of the armchair and over to the smoked glass wall cabinet for an ashtray.

I slowly stirred the sugar in the cups, wanting to ram the spoon down Majid's throat. I wondered what his reaction would be if he knew I was in the army, yomping a rucksack up a hill and eating out of a mess tin. The thought made my mouth curl up at the ends.

I noticed Majid's wife hadn't touched the cup of tea I'd put in front of her. Behind those dark glasses I had no idea who she was looking at, but I'd decided she didn't like me. Her arms were plastered in gold bangles so I knew that status and appearance were her two driving factors. Every now and then, her head would twitch towards Mum's homemade curtains and matching cushions.

Majid waved a match out, caught in time by an ashtray Mum was holding, then he wrapped his fingers around the cigarette like a hookah and puffed a cloud of blue smoke into the clean air.

'And Kashif?' Mum coughed – she was standing above him. 'Does your son have a degree?'

Majid took a long drag before making the announcement. 'My Kashif runs the family business with me.'

'Business.' Mum's eyes sparkled across the room at Dad who was still gazing out of the window. 'Very good. What business is that?'

'We own two market stalls selling ladies' fashion shoes. I run one enterprise at Ashton market and my son runs the other in Rochdale.'

Majid turned and smacked my dad on his back. 'So, brother, are you a businessman?'

Dad cleared his throat. 'Well,' he began, 'we have the kebab shop next door and I run a butcher's shop…'

'These samosas have come fresh from the shop.' Mum pointed at the empty plate. 'Last week I invented a new curry which is hotter than a vindaloo.'

Majid looked impressed. 'What is it called?'

'Tindaloo.'

I began to gather the empty plates to fill the uncomfortable silence.

'Are you thinking of expanding your butcher business?' Majid asked Dad, stubbing the cigarette out and lighting another.

'Well … there is a mini store next door run by a Hindi man…'

Majid cracked up his laugher, rising to hyena pitch. 'You should offer him a piece of cow meat from your shop. That will get him out.'

Dad looked over at Mum then back at Majid. 'We

get on well. Better than our Bangladeshi friends back in the factory days. The war was going on over there, and here we wouldn't speak to each other.'

Majid nodded. 'Yes ... tough times.' Majid took another drag on his cigarette. 'It's all that Bhutto's fault. If he hadn't been elected we'd still own East Pakistan. Thank goodness his daughter was thrown out otherwise she'd have given the rest away to that Bush man.'

'Benazir is a very clever woman,' Mum said. 'Oxford-educated, I hear.'

Dad spoke softly. 'When I was fourteen, I was handed a gun and put on the front line, not knowing whether I would live or die. These days, all the youth care about is who made their trainers.'

I looked at up Dad, feeling frustrated that I couldn't tell him about my other world. *I understand you!* I wanted to scream out.

'They'll soon find out when they get married.' Majid glanced round at his son who was now looking down at his hands. 'A clip round the ear hole will sort them out. I saw something on telly the other day where American children were taking their parents to court for disciplining them. Can you believe it? Allah knows what our grandchildren will turn out like...'

I closed my eyes to his noise and thought back to the training. The next phase was the hills. I was petrified,

petrified of failing. This regiment was now a part of me. It was where I belonged. It wasn't just about earning a sandy beret; it meant so much more. It would mark a great leap forward, change people's views on religion, gender and the future role of the Special Forces, and I was not giving up even if it killed me.

CHAPTER ONE

NORTHERN BEGINNINGS

MY FATHER DIED three days after New Year in January 2011. I'd received a call from Pakistan in the early hours of the morning. I thought I'd be hysterical, have a breakdown or at least be sad. Instead, I put the phone down and went out to do my weekly shopping at the local supermarket.

I couldn't figure out exactly what I was feeling until I got back, and then I realised what it was: regret. Regret that I'd never told him who I really was or what I had become. Would he have been proud that I'd followed in his footsteps, or disappointed that I'd not fulfilled the daughter role? But none of this mattered any more as I would never know.

My father's death brought back flickers of my childhood. Dad came over to England in the 1960s, as a veteran of the British Indian Army and a soldier for the Pakistani Army during the 1947 partition. He was fourteen when he joined the army. He made his friends there and then watched them be killed one by one. He hardly spoke of his time in the military, other than the lethal roles given to soldiers during the war of Pakistan's Independence, where they had to stuff grenades into the smocks of their buddy soldiers selected to be thrown under a tank of four enemy soldiers.

My three brothers were born in Pakistan and they came over with Mum once Dad could afford reasonable accommodation to raise a family with money earned from his job in the cotton factory. Then my sister and I were born here. I was the youngest of five.

I grew up in a two-up two-down, accommodating seven of us. The front room was south facing and had the sun coming through all day, but it was only ever opened for guests, mainly men. It smelt of plastic and the only noise came from kids playing out on the front street. The three-piece sofa set looked like it had hardly been sat on, the coffee table was covered in an embroidered white tablecloth in case it got dusty and the black and white television sat in the corner of the room was never switched on in case it broke.

The women who visited would sit in the back room with their kids. It was dark with broken furniture and conveniently situated next to the kitchen so it smelt of curry all the time. We didn't have to worry about spilling anything on the carpet or being slapped if we scribbled on the walls. The window looked out onto the backyard, which was always shady and only ever used to hang washing out.

Bath time for me was in the kitchen sink; even beyond the baby stage, owing to my physical stature. Mum would fill it up then lift my small body up and sit me on the draining board to scrub me with soap. On the few occasions she fell ill, Dad took over. He would get impatient with the soap slipping off my bony legs and arms and squirt washing-up liquid over me instead.

The sleeping arrangements were a little complicated. My three brothers shared one room and my parents shared the other with my sister and me. There were two beds in my parents' room: my sister and mum slept together, and I slept with my dad.

When I was five, Dad changed shifts in the factory to nights. Up until then I had taken his presence for granted.

'Where's Dad?' I'd ask, as soon as I'd get home from school. Then I'd go upstairs and notice the main bedroom door closed and his snores coming through.

His new routine left a big hole in my life; after school, he was no longer due back from work but upstairs asleep. And when I woke up in the morning, he was still out at work.

I would see his mysterious figure floating around the house on a Sunday. Occasionally I heard my parents have their differences in the kitchen. My dad was quietly spoken and Mum would respond with big drama. I would listen behind the door and silently cheer Dad on. He was always right.

Islam was never forced upon us, but it naturally became part of our lives growing up. It was something to respect, like our parents. Sometimes a religious figure would visit the house wearing a big hat with a title of Hajji or Hafiz. On these occasions, all hell broke loose. Mum would run around the house like a headless chicken tidying up, then cook up a special biryani crammed with meat in a big pan and serve it up in her best crockery to the guest. Then she would stand to one side of the small kitchen table (wearing her headscarf extra tight) and watch Dad and the guest eat, waiting on them.

'Islam is very important for children, especially growing up in this country,' the big hat would say, pointing a finger in the air.

'We agree,' Mum would pipe up from behind.

However, the big hat was not interested in Mum's opinion. He would stare at Dad until he got the acknowledgment he needed. This would sometimes take a while, as Dad was a controlled man and didn't feel the need to rush to tell people his thoughts.

'A good education and work ethic is just as important,' he'd finally point out.

'No, no…' the big hat would bite back, booming his voice to remind my parents who had the authority around here. 'Islam gives a child everything. This is where they will get education and work.'

Dad would just go along with it; sometimes eating quickly so Mum would serve up the chai and the guest would leave. He wasn't interested in religious debates. His priority was to buy a bigger house one day and have his own business; he had ambitions that these religious figureheads didn't understand.

When these visits occurred, I would have to stay upstairs in the bedroom with my sister until the guest left. Just witnessing my mum's behaviour made their presence a daunting one. Little did I know at the time that one of these figures would later become my imam.

I was six when my mum made me attend mosque after school. The closest to our house was a Bangladeshi one, situated above a parade of dilapidated shops on a busy road, with a dimly lit narrow staircase leading up to the prayer room. It had green woodchip wallpaper and smelt of stale curry. The room was laid out with rows of low benches; girls sat on one side and boys on the other.

I hated it. The kids would take the mick out of me because I was Pakistani. They spoke in their own language so I couldn't understand them. The war between Pakistan and Bangladesh was long since over, but their parents still carried it in their hearts and these kids had picked up on that. My mum couldn't see this.

'We all come from the same piece of cloth,' she would say.

To her the war was about a bunch of men on both sides of the border with big egos. The war had only lasted nine months, but it was brutal. This was never explained to me, though, and it left me bemused at why the other kids in the mosque hated me so much.

The Bangladeshi imam spoke to me in Urdu so we could communicate. Originally, the language was pushed by Jinnah, the founder of Pakistan, as the product of Islamic culture across Pakistan, but failed because the majority of Pakistanis spoke Punjabi. Nowadays, Urdu is the language used in Indian movies to reach a wider audience of Indians, Pakistanis and Bangladeshis.

My imam was an old chap, bent over with a hump

on his back, a wiry grey beard and eyes that watered all the time. He wore a long white tunic that looked like it had never seen an iron, and baggy trousers. He sat cross-legged on the floor between the boys and girls, a stack of canes behind him, watching us like a hawk. We kept our heads down, reading aloud and filling the room with noise.

'Louder,' he would chant. 'So Allah can hear you and forgive you.'

My hand would reach up and pull my headscarf over my forehead, to cover any hair that might be showing. It was my first experience of wearing a scarf and it made me feel grown up.

Every so often, the imam would turn around to his stack of canes and choose one with his bony fingers. The short, thick ones were used on the hand and the long, thin ones were for both hands and feet, which he could strike at a distance.

Occasionally I experienced the long thin cane for spending too long on the toilet when I had constipation. The toilet was the backyard shed; a hole in the ground, no lighting, and stank to high heaven. I would hold my breath and squat down, clutching the hem of my trousers so that they wouldn't become soiled. When I got out, there was a queue of angry Bangladeshi kids snaking back to the building. By the time I walked back up the stairs to the prayer room, I knew I was in trouble.

Slowly, I stepped forward towards the imam and stopped a few feet away from him, holding my hand out. I knew the drill; I'd seen other kids do it when they were in trouble, but that didn't stop my heart from pounding.

'You know why you are getting this,' the imam would say. Then he would tap the end of the cane in the centre of my palm to ensure a good shot, then raise it to the ceiling and strike down, full force.

The first strike of the cane set my skin on fire. Tears streamed down my face but no sound came out of my mouth, as it would only earn me an extra one. The second strike numbed me. Every kid in the room was staring at me; some smirking, some trying to look sorry, and some amazed at my stupidity. The pain and broken skin would soon go away but the humiliation stayed. I couldn't tell anyone at home; challenging an imam's actions was unheard of, especially in my mum's world.

To make matters more challenging, we had to learn the Koran in Arabic, the holy language, which meant we didn't understand the words. I couldn't understand the logic behind why it was done this way. I would get through it much faster if it were translated in English – and there was the added benefit that I would understand what I was reading.

I wanted to leave but there was no shortcut. My parents wouldn't allow me to leave until I finished reading the whole Koran in Arabic.

'You are not a full Muslim until it's completed,' Mum's blanket expression would be.

'What was that supposed to mean?' I wanted to retort. 'I don't understand what a Muslim is because I don't understand what I'm reading!'

The months dragged, the girls in my group moved on to join the bigger girls and receive a copy of the Koran, while I still stayed at the beginners' area struggling with the alphabet booklet.

My daily routine started well in the mornings with school, which I enjoyed, but by 3 p.m. my heart palpitations kicked in and I started to dread the evening at mosque. I would get home from primary school, eat a butter sandwich Mum had made from the scarce ingredients in the fridge, grab my scarf and booklet and off I'd go.

I couldn't speak to my siblings about it, especially my sister. She was ten and the golden girl, recently awarded a prayer mat by the imam at the same mosque for winning a religious competition. Mum was cooing to everyone about it and, to my dismay, this created a benchmark for me.

I despised my sister's intelligence, religious articulation

and all the attention she got from Dad because of the good school reports she was getting. The older we got, the more she blossomed, while I remained small, dark and skinny, which was regarded as unattractive in the Pakistani community. I was sick of being in her shadow, but had a feeling this was just the start.

My brothers were teenagers by now and occasionally took me out to play. It pleased Mum no end that they showed an interest in their little sister and encouraged me to get some fresh air.

They'd park their home-made go-kart at the top of a big hill and put me inside, then give it a big push. Mouth open, eyes bulging, I flew down. As the cold wind hit my face, I screamed the Lord's Prayer recited at school assembly, which then morphed into a couple of letters of the Arabic alphabet: 'Our father in heaven ... lead us not into temptation ... Bismillah ... Allaaaaaaah Wakhbar!'

Somehow I'd survive, after I'd hit a bollard and went crashing at an angle.

Another game my brothers played with me was called 'bundling me up in a sleeping bag', which was usually played when Mum and Dad were out. At first, I used to panic in the dark confined space, as the air became thin and I was unable to breathe. The smell of cheesy feet and my voice echoing in my ears became all too much. However, over time, I learnt to remain calm, take only snippets of air until one of my brothers untied the knot and allowed my lungs to fill up with oxygen. Soon I got sick of them and wanted to play on my own.

The caning at the mosque was getting me down. It became a regular occurrence, not giving my skin enough time to heal. Kids sat away from me in case they were tarnished with the same brush by the imam, forming a big floor space around me.

It began to affect my schooling. No longer did I find school fun. I would stand on my own at playtime waiting for the bell to go so I could go back in. Sometimes I would see my sister on the other side of the courtyard where the primary school pupils played, surrounded by a gang of girls. Quickly I would hide behind a wall, watching her discreetly. I didn't want her to see my flaws or tell my parents that I couldn't do what came so naturally to her.

After school, I would wait for her so we could go home together, but she was always preoccupied with her friends. Quietly I followed behind until we reached the top of our street, where the girls left us and I would have my sister all to myself for the three-minute walk down to the house.

One day as I walked across the croft to mosque I

decided to follow my heart. I'm not going, I told myself. Everybody hated me and I hated them, including the imam, so what's the point, I thought.

Instead, I went to hang out at the secondary school across the road, which was closed by this time. I looked up at the high gates not sure how to get to the other side, then stepped forward and began to clamber up, clutching my alphabet book tight in one hand and wedging my buckled shoes between the bars to help me over.

On the first few attempts, my hands slid down the bars causing me to fall back and jolt my knees. I was not giving up. Besides, I was late for mosque and was not going to risk a caning for that. On my fourth attempt, I managed to pull my body over the top bar and drop down the other side.

The slippery soles of my shoes missed the ground, causing me to land on my hands and knees. I could feel the skin burn beneath my polyester trousers, but it didn't matter. From the ground, I scanned the surroundings: the empty buildings, netball courts and car park. It was strangely quiet and, for a moment, I became worried that I shouldn't have been there. But it was the right decision. This is my new life, I thought excitedly. No more mosques, no horrible kids and no more caning. Happily I got up, wiped the grit off my hands and skipped through the courtyard, feeling a weight lift off my chest. I couldn't stop smiling and twirling; I was almost tripping over myself.

I wondered if this feeling of freedom was what every English kid on our street had. The ones that were allowed to play rather than pray after school; the ones who looked different from me.

My thoughts were interrupted by a group of boys who appeared from around the corner of a concrete building. They wore monkey boots and green bomber jackets and had shaved heads. I couldn't make out their faces because they were stuck inside small polythene bags that they were breathing in and out of.

One of them spotted me.

'Paki!' he shouted, making the others look round and head towards me.

I'd heard that word being directed towards people with brown skin like me but didn't know what it meant, just that it wasn't nice. Before I knew what was going on, they started running towards me with angry faces and veins bulging out of their necks. I didn't know what I had done to get them so angry but decided to leg it away from them as fast as I could.

Tears sprang to my eyes. I clutched my trousers that kept coming down because of the loose elastic Mum had put in the waist. Perhaps this was the punishment the imam had kept going on about if we did something wrong. This was my punishment for not going to mosque.

I ran across the netball court and, thankfully, the gate was open on the other side. I didn't dare look behind. I had visions of a boy grabbing the hood of my coat and the zipper choking me to death. I looked around, losing sense of direction. All the buildings looked the same. Frantically, I searched between each one for the gate, for the boys, for a way out. Finally, I found a gate. I didn't know if it was the right one and I didn't care. Kicking hard against the bars, I lifted myself up. I didn't care about the pain (nothing came close to the imam's caning) – I just had to get out of there. I jumped down the other side of the gate and sprinted down to my street.

The skies darkened above. It felt later than the time I normally returned from mosque. My mind raced for excuses to give at home but I couldn't think of any. I imagined Mum worried sick, thinking I'd been run over by a truck and getting Dad out of bed to go and find me.

It made me run faster, wanting to stop them worrying. I slowed down as I got close to the house, calming my breath, relieved to be on safe territory. I imagined them stood inside waiting for me and opening their arms for a hug, glad to see me alive.

I spotted Dad's silhouette in the front room through the net curtains as I walked up the garden path. He was sat with someone, which was strange for this time in the evening. Before I had a chance to knock, the front door was flung open. Mum's face looked down at me like thunder.

'I'm sorry, Amma,' I quickly offered, following her inside. 'The imam had us reading very late tonight and I ran back as quickly as I could—'

'Where's your scarf?' she interjected with a stern tone.

I touched the crown of my head, racking my brains. It must have fallen off during the chase. I was not going back to find it.

'You were reading so hard your headscarf fell off?' Mum offered.

I opened my mouth to tell her I'd left it in the lobby of the mosque when I put my shoes back on but she got in before me.

'You are so good at reading you don't need your book any more?'

My heart skipped a beat as I looked down at my grazed hands. I must have dropped it when running across the netball court as I pulled the elastic up on my trousers.

'I left them both at mosque, Amma,' I blurted. 'I'll bring them back home tomorrow.'

Mum didn't respond; she just stared at me. I couldn't figure it out, then suddenly the front-room door opened and Dad came out, followed by the imam. *My* imam.

I couldn't believe he was here with my dad putting up a united front against me. I wanted to tell Dad not to believe anything the imam may have told him about me not being at mosque tonight because it wasn't true. But Dad didn't even look at me. Instead, he turned his back on me and left the house with the imam.

Panicked, I ran to the kitchen where Mum had disappeared. I cared less what she thought, but she was the only way to my dad. I could hear voices inside and pressed my ear on the door. My heart slumped as I recognised Auntie Pataani's voice. I couldn't stand her. She was fat, loud and stank of coconut oil. She wasn't my real aunt, thank God, but a friend of Mum's who I had to call 'Auntie'.

I imagined her sat on her big bum, feet up on the pouffe, stuffing her face with samosas and gossiping about everyone. Her nickname was 'Telephone Box' because she spent her days cruising around town looking for Pakistani girls wrongfully out of school, then she would dive into the nearest telephone box and ring their parents.

'Thoba Thoba,' I heard her say through the door. This was her way of warding off the 'evil spirit' that had got into me and was causing me to behave in such a way. 'That is terrible news about your daughter. No parent should have to go through this. Where does she get it from?'

My mum began giving her a rundown of all the women in Dad's family.

'You always get one that takes after the mother and one taking after the father,' she told Mum wisely. 'Your other daughter has taken after you, of course. She is a very good girl.'

'I don't know what to do with this one,' my mum said in crisis mode, 'she's trouble.'

I clutched the doorknob tight. *No, I'm not!*

Mum carried on: 'The school have already complained that she hit a boy on the head with a rounders' bat...'

That's because he called me curry breath.

'I buy her pretty clips to wear in her hair and she swaps them in the playground for sweets then comes home and tells me she lost them.'

How did she know that?

'Thoba Thoba ... you need to be careful she doesn't get a boyfriend next,' Auntie Pataani assisted.

I don't like boys!

I wanted to barge in and tell them both that I'd heard everything but knew if I did it would only make Mum more angry for disrespecting my elders. Worse still, it would give Auntie Pataani more ammunition to get Mum fired up. I had never seen eye-to-eye with that woman in my short life and wished she would go away or just die. Mum missed her family that she'd left behind in Pakistan, especially her sisters, and Auntie Pataani was a comfortable placeholder to share all her concerns with, especially those about me.

From that day on, things changed. Mum would take me to mosque every day and pick me up. Dad didn't talk to me, but to be fair I was so embarrassed that I was avoiding him.

Soon after, when I got to primary school, we moved house into a very English area. In those days, ethnic festivities were not recognised in schools. We didn't get a day off for Eid and nor did we get halal meat. If the school dinner was meat pie and beetroot, we ate the beetroot and left the pie. No big dramas were made, though it did put me off beetroot for life. The same went for prayers in assembly; everyone joined in. There was no big discussion about being from one faith or another, we all recited the Lord's Prayer and believed that one day we would go to heaven if we were good.

Our parents never allowed us to take a day off school. The thought of their children 'lounging' in bed while others learnt something wasn't acceptable in our house. The few times I became ill, Dad made me sprint up and down the stairs ten times, and then sent me to school. Perhaps it was that it got my blood flow going, but I did feel better.

To my dismay, I still had to attend mosque, but this time it was a Pakistani one a bus ride away. It was the pain of my life and turned out to be even worse than the previous one. The girls were cliquey. I was ostracised because I didn't live in the community and they asked me loads of questions as a result. 'Which mosque did you come from?' the gang leader demanded. She was a tall, specky girl with a pale complexion.

'The Bangladeshi one,' I replied.

'Pooooh!' The girls pinched their noses and screwed up their faces to indicate that Bangladeshis smelt.

'You look like a Bengali as well.' They laughed their heads off.

I didn't find it funny, especially because I knew they were right. I had similar problems at school, as I was the only non-white there. My parents didn't see it as an issue, and if they did, they never showed it. It did bother the familiar skinheads hanging outside the school gate, however, which were growing in numbers. I once made the mistake of walking straight through them, still wondering why they'd chased me, why they didn't like me and whether there was any way I could be friends with them. I smiled at one as I passed and, the next thing I knew, a beer bottle hit the back of my head, making me feel dizzy. I fled as fast as I could, the noisy traffic drowning out their laughter the further away I got.

I was hot and panicked, firstly because my legs were sweaty under the three pairs of woolly tights I wore to make my ankles look fatter under the frilly dresses Mum made me wear, also because of the horrible smell of alcohol coming from my fashionable side ponytail, which I hoped would be gone by the time I got home. I couldn't talk to anyone about it. My brothers had left home by this time and my sister was at secondary school. If I tried to approach Mum she would blame me for not crossing the road by the lollipop lady and walking on the other side.

Dad had now taken the plunge and left the factory, putting his minimal savings into starting up a halal butcher's shop on the other side of town. He worked seven days a week and got home late in the evenings so I only caught a brief glimpse of him before going to bed. Soon he began to take half a day off on Sundays because he couldn't take any more of Mum's nagging to spend some time at home with us. So this was when I was able to see him, and on these days he taught me how to play chess. A strange way for father and daughter to bond in our community, but it was his way. After we moved, Mum became even more house-proud. She would buzz away on the sewing machine all day making curtains, cushions, tablecloths, quilt covers and anything else she could think of to make the place more stylish.

It looked like a showroom and for the guests it became a topic of conversation trying to guess what additions had been made since their last visit.

My main focus now was on settling into my new school. For some reason Mum became flustered over the lunch arrangements and kept switching from 'home for dinner' to 'packed lunch'. School dinners was not an option, they were too expensive. Dad's income from the shop came just over the threshold for subsidies on school meals. At school, a small table was set in the corner of the dining hall seating the eight pupils with packed lunches.

The first day I wedged myself between two girls at the table with my large Tupperware box and peeled the lid open. Suddenly everyone stopped talking and looked round. The smell of my mother's fried onions and garlic in the spicy omelette filled the air. She insisted I had it every day because, according to her, the eggs would help me to grow taller. I insisted she put it between two slices of bread to make it look like a sandwich and more like the rest of the lunches around the table.

'What's that?' the girl sitting beside me asked. She wrinkled her nose, staring down at the two slices of Sunblest white bread in my hand.

'Sandwich,' I replied quietly, clearing my throat and starting to feel my face burn. The sandwich was very tasty. I loved my mum's cooking, but right then I would have preferred to eat dry bread if it meant I could avoid this unwanted attention. A part of me wanted to offer the girl a bite, but knew it would raise more questions and I would have to explain its ingredients. I started eating the sandwich quickly, hoping the smell of boiled cabbage drifting from the kitchens would kill off the curry smell. The girl turned the other way and began talking to someone else.

My eyes wandered around the big hall. Each table was set out like a family; two monitors at the head acting as Mum and Dad and serving up and passing the plates of chocolate cake and mint custard down the table. I'd never experienced a family meal at home because Dad was always out at work and Mum was too busy. She'd recently got a 'piece-work machinist' job to do from home. The work came from the local textile factory and allowed her to get some extra money to pay the bills until Dad's business got better. She would sit at the sewing machine after serving dinner until we went to bed.

To my surprise, the girl turned back to me and introduced herself as Julie Gordon. She had short, ginger, curly hair, very pale, freckled skin, a snotty nose and smelt to high heaven – as if she had never had a bath. She was a big, tough girl who played for 'Team A' netball.

Due to my height, I was put on Team B. I was a reserve for Team A, though I dreaded the day any member got ill and I had to take their place. The girls were massive and playing similar opponents was a scary thought.

Unfortunately, that day came and, worse still, it was a tournament. It was a crisp winter's day and we were playing an away game against a local Catholic school. I wore two pairs of socks under my netball skirt, crinkled down to avoid the girls laughing at my skinny ankles. I scouted for my opponent in a matching 'GA' (Goal Attack) bib but in a different colour. I spotted her; she was twice my size – in both directions. She was built like the Incredible Hulk and I swear she was even blocking the sun when she took her position in front of me.

The whistle blew: we were off, and the noise began.

Julie was playing centre. She tried chucking the ball at me a few times but this girl didn't need to move much to defend. I imagined her laughing over my head as the ball kept on coming my way and she caught it and threw it to one of her team. I was so cross I wanted to kick her bum but knew I'd be thrown off court and let my team down.

By some fluke, I managed to wriggle underneath one of her big arms and could finally see sunshine and my team again. She may have been bigger and stronger, but I could run faster.

There was a great buzz around the team, the momentum was up and I was getting smiles from Julie.

The girl muttered something at me under her breath that I didn't catch. I replayed the muffled words back in my head and realised she had called me 'stupid paki'. It felt like a punch in my stomach. She did it for effect and it worked. The ball kept coming my way, but I was too scared to catch it in case she said something horrible again. Eventually my team stopped trying with me.

We lost the match. I felt like a failure, weak and embarrassed to be part of the elite team. I picked up my sports bag and stood by the edge of the netball court, watching Julie centre court surrounded by the team. Eventually she broke away and walked over to me. I wanted to tell her what had happened with that girl on court, but didn't want her to think I was using it as an excuse for losing the tournament.

To my surprise, Julie didn't mention anything about the game but invited me for 'tea' at her house after netball practice the next day. I wasn't expecting such a kind offer and couldn't turn it down if I was to stay friends with her. She was my only friend and my only way of staying on Team A. I accepted the invitation then walked to the bus stop.

The bus shelter was crowded. People huddled inside to avoid the blustery, cold wind that had suddenly risen from nowhere. I sat down on the pavement, leaning against a wall with my legs stretched out in front. I kept thinking of an excuse to give Mum about going to Julie's tomorrow. It wasn't worth telling her the truth, because she would make a big drama out if it and insist on coming with me. However, even that wasn't as worrying as having to return the invitation back to my house. This would mean asking Mum to make chips instead of chapatti and eating with knives and forks instead of our hands.

My thoughts were interrupted by two teenage boys riding up on their bikes and stopping in front of my legs.

'Move it!' one of them spat.

I looked up at them and suddenly got a flashback of the netball girl, making the Julie problem fizzle out. I knew they expected the same reaction as her. They wanted me to cower, pull my legs into my chest and apologise to them. Just the thought was making me angry.

'No,' I replied, looking beyond my feet at the two feet of paving space. 'There is plenty of room to go round. And you shouldn't be riding your bikes on the pavement.' I recalled an incident with a police officer outside my house telling someone to get off their bike and walk.

They were visibly shocked and exchanged glances. 'Fuckin' move,' the other joined in.

'No,' I repeated. They would have to cycle over my legs before I was going to move.

The people queuing under the bus shelter pretended not to notice and quickly shuffled forward as the bus arrived. This got me angrier. I didn't want to get up and be defeated, but at the same time I really couldn't wait for another bus and be left with these boys. I stayed focused on the queue, waiting for the last person to get on, then shot up and ran over. The door closed just as I got there. I looked in, staring at the driver with pleading eyes. Thankfully he could see what was going on and opened up.

I stepped inside, headed over to a window seat and searched for the boys as the bus pulled away. My tolerance level was about to burst. I'd had enough of everything going on in my life.

Perhaps I wasn't meant to fight back. I couldn't imagine my parents or siblings behaving this way, though I'm sure they had experienced something similar but it was never discussed at home.

As the bus stopped at the traffic lights, the boys rode past and looked in. I knew they were looking for me, but what could they do? I was protected by the pane of glass between us.

I felt anger build up inside me and I stuck two fingers up at them. I knew it was wrong, but I felt a rush of liberation, and revenge on the netball girl. A few passengers looked at me in disbelief, especially the elderly blue-rinse brigade. I looked back with a hard stare, wanting to ask why, when the boys insulted me, I was ignored, but when I retaliated I received surprise?

I went home with the further worry that the boys would be waiting for me next time. I racked my brains for a solution. A few things came to mind: I could skip the bus and run home instead, which would make me late but I would save on the fare and be able to buy chewies from the sweet shop. Alternatively, I could hide in the queue at the bus stop and hope they didn't see me. Or, as a last resort, I could take Mum's air freshener and spray it on their eyes if they said anything to me again. I wasn't set on any of the options, but one thing was for sure: I wasn't taking it any more.

The next day I went to Julie's house after netball practice. It was small, like our first house, and set on a side street away from traffic, unlike ours, which was on a busy road.

It was strange going to an English person's house. Firstly, it smelt different, not of the usual garlicky smell of our house but more 'bready'. Her mum, Beryl, welcomed me with a big smile. Her hairstyle was like something out of the '60s, a beehive with curly brown locks down the sides of her round face. There was another woman, heavily pregnant, sat on the sofa who looked like her twin, except for the hairdo, so I guessed it was her sister. Julie also had a big brother. He was fat and introduced himself with a 'hiya'. What I wasn't expecting was a big dog in the house. Those rabies adverts on TV were going round in my head and I had almost been bitten by a dog on the way home from school recently. It was big and black and could smell my fear. It chased me around the block and wouldn't go away so I had to knock on the door of one of the houses and get the people living there to shoo it away.

Beryl assured me their dog wouldn't bite, but his barking was telling me different. Reluctantly they locked him up in the kitchen when I refused to come inside.

To my surprise 'tea' was not 'egg and chips' but a meat dish. I sat at the kitchen table with Julie and stared down at my plate, not wanting to say I couldn't eat it because it wasn't halal and doubly worried it was pork, which would make me puke. I remembered a prayer the imam taught us, reciting the first line of the Koran three times, before starting a meal. Perhaps if I said that it would make everything on my plate halal. I convinced myself this was the case, closed my eyes and tried to remember how the words went.

Beryl thought it was sweet that I was praying before eating my food and offered me another helping because

I had finished first. It was intentional. I had swallowed big chunks so my taste buds did not savour the meat. I politely took another helping, trying to keep the first lot down by gulping lots of water. The meal was followed by dessert, something we didn't get at home, but which thankfully didn't have to be prayed over.

I began to relax, savouring the sweet ice cream in my mouth for as long as possible. It was nice being in an English house, but I did wonder where her dad was. Perhaps he was working like mine.

I glanced up at the small kitchen window; it was getting dark and Mum would be worried. I'd told her I would be a bit late because of a double netball session. Surprisingly she didn't question it, which was good as I'd be able to use the excuse again.

'Don't worry.' Beryl looked across at Julie's brother, who was sat in front of the telly eating a plate of chips, 'Gary will walk you back.'

'No, no … it's okay,' I stopped her. If Mum saw me come home with a boy, she'd kill me and Auntie Pataani would have a field day dissecting the situation with her.

However, Beryl wasn't having it – I was her responsibility until I got home safe. I looked at Julie, who was now in her slippers and getting her homework out. Reluctantly I put my duffel coat on and headed out with Gary.

It must have been the longest fifteen minutes of my life walking home with him. Not a word was passed between us. I wondered if he had learning difficulties, but wondered more what would happen when we got to my house. I looked down at the paving, tinged orange by the streetlamps above, and mulled over my options.

'This is my house,' I said, pointing at a terraced house a block away from mine. 'You can go now.'

He looked bemused as there were no lights on inside, then finally spoke. 'I'll see you in,' he said, blowing his fingers through his woollen gloves and hopping one foot to the other. The cold wind had also made my fingers and toes tingle but there were more pressing issues occupying me right now. Perhaps he wants to come in and get warm, I thought, panicking all of a sudden. Of course, if it was Julie there would be no problem, nor would I be standing outside the wrong house.

I shook my head profusely then waved at his big round face until he walked back up the street. I waited until he was a dot in the distance then ran down to my house.

Mum had left me a plate of dhal on the kitchen table, thinking I hadn't eaten. She told me off for being very late, which I was expecting. Once she'd got it out of her system, I asked if my netball friend could come for tea and if we could have chips. She looked at me like

I had three heads and responded by reminding me of 'our way' and the 'English way', which meant we were having chapattis.

I was sick of all these rules; first it was the 'Muslim way', then 'the girls' way' and now 'the English way'. How many more barriers were going to be put up? My mum had no idea what it was like for me. She was illiterate. She'd never attended school or sat in a mixed-gender classroom. She'd never known what it was like to do everything different from the other kids.

Defeated, the next day I tried to think of excuses to give Julie for not coming over to my house, but each one sounded lame and thoughtless. As a kid, the logic of English food served at an English house and Asian food served at an Asian house didn't occur to me. I just wanted to be like the rest of the kids at school and this cuisine was making me feel different, more so than my physical appearance.

The invitation was finally returned. Julie and I walked to my house after netball practice one evening. The cold temperature had made the snow settle into bumpy ice on the ground, making me slip and slide as I led the way.

I spent the whole time trying to romanticise my family to her; the traditional clothes Mum wore, the language we spoke and the food we ate, all the time avoiding using the word 'different'.

Julie's reaction was difficult to gauge – not surprised, excited or phased. I suddenly got worried she would relay all this back to the girls at school tomorrow, especially the netball ones, but it was too late – we were almost home.

Mum welcomed Julie at the door in her pigeon English. 'Hello, Juuli … come here.' She opened the door wider to let her in.

Mum wore a lime-green shalwar kameez, with yellow embroidery edging the dupatta that was loosely placed over her head. She wriggled her maroon toenails that were sticking out of her red clogs. It didn't matter what season it was outside or what colour combination she was wearing, she never took those clogs off.

Julie's red hair glowed in the dark hallway as she stepped inside. It looked strange to have an English person in the house. We stood in a triangle. I could smell the curry cooking in the kitchen at the back of the house and wondered if I should say something or let Julie guess what we were having tonight.

Mum started giggling. It was one of her traits when she didn't know what to say, which was not very often. However, speaking English meant she had to think up the words to say. Finally, she turned to me and told me in Punjabi what curry we were having tonight and to tell Julie in English.

'What she say?' Julie eyes flitted between us, then she laughed uncontrollably. It must have sounded strange to her, almost cartoony.

I felt my face burn as I translated, then Mum cut in with another reel of Punjabi to tell us to wash our hands.

I didn't want to take Julie to the bathroom in case she questioned the *lota* by the toilet. I would then have to explain that it was used to wash the private parts before praying. Instead, I led her straight into the kitchen to eat.

We passed the living room, where Dad was glued to the telly watching the news on the Falklands War. I wanted to go in and introduce Julie and tell him she was in the A stream at school. I stopped myself, though, remembering that I had told him I was also in the A stream, when really I was in C. I couldn't tell him the truth, not now my sister was coming home with A*s. This secret wasn't a problem until I got my report at the end of the year.

The only thing that had impressed him so far was that I'd beaten him at chess a few times. He'd never say it but I could tell from the glint in his eyes. It meant so much to me because I knew he saw chess as an intelligent person's game, and that small recognition from him made my world make sense again.

Julie and I sat at the kitchen table. I looked round and suddenly noticed Mum had laid out an odd set of crockery for Julie; the special set for English people who came to the house, as she would describe it. Her explanation was, because they ate pig, they couldn't use the halal plates. Julie's face said it all, questioning why her plate and glass were different to the rest. She opened her mouth to say something just as Mum nuzzled between us and poured curry into our bowls with a ladle then placed a basket of chapattis for us to share on the table.

Julie was even more confused when Mum handed her a saucer of sliced oranges to squeeze over the curry to sweeten the taste, a trick Mum used with me when I was very young. Then she came and sat on the spare chair and smiled at Julie, resting her elbows on the table. Julie looked at me, then back at Mum. Of course, it was different at Julie's house; her mum ate dinner with us, not just serve and wait. I knew it was just a cultural difference, but it was bothering me.

I quickly led the way by ripping a piece of chapatti and making a spoon out of it to scoop the curry sauce. Julie followed. It was all very hard work. Firstly, Mum couldn't have a conversation with us like Beryl could, because she kept switching to Punjabi and asking me to translate, then Julie got frustrated trying to scoop the curry and eventually asked for a fork. This put Mum on the back foot as we didn't use forks in the house and she didn't know what one was. She now had to find some more 'non-halal cutlery' and ended up offering Julie a rather large dessert spoon that had been at the bottom of the drawer for ages.

Then, even with the orange juice squeezed in the curry, the chillies hit the back of Julie's throat and she grappled for the goblet of water.

Mum panicked. She got up to refill the glass of water, asking me in Punjabi if she was OK. Her voice got louder, as did the noise from her clogs. Julie began coughing uncontrollably. I patted her back as she tried to say something. Her hair was all over the place, eyes watering, and her face bright red. Meanwhile, Mum was bouncing around the cupboards trying to find a solution. She came back with a bowl of sugar and tried to shove a spoonful into Julie's mouth. Julie didn't know what was happening until she moved the tiny crystals around with her tongue. Then she stopped coughing and just sat quietly, staring at the sugar bowl.

The meal ended when Dad came in, probably to figure out what all the noise was about. He stood between us making polite conversation with Julie in English, which I was thankful for, then left the kitchen holding a cup of chai Mum had handed him.

I smiled at Julie, pleased that something had eventually gone right, and took a sip of water.

Julie smiled back. 'Is that your granddad?' she asked.

The glass missed my mouth and water trickled down my chin onto my netball skirt. I couldn't believe she'd said that and I felt a sudden rage set in. No one had *ever* said that, nor had it occurred to me before that my dad was probably twice as old as most of the parents at my school. Perhaps the teachers thought my brother was my dad when he attended parents' evening in the place of Dad, who worked late, and Mum, who couldn't understand English.

I responded with a poker face. He may be older, I wanted to tell her, but he was the best dad in the world. He was my universe.

The next morning, school started with geography. I hated the subject. Who cares where Gambia is located, I thought. It wasn't as if I was ever going to go there.

I sat at the back of the class with Julie, studying a map together. The teacher, Miss Wilcox, was stood at the front. She had the most boring monotone voice. I tried to concentrate on what she was saying but kept thinking about Julie.

We'd hardly had a chance to talk about the evening. I did try to spark up a conversation during registration but she avoided eye contact. My paranoia kicked in when I noticed a few girls looking round at us during class and wondered if she had told them anything.

Julie turned the page over to a map of Chile and studied its strange shape and population data.

'Did you like coming to my house yesterday?' I
whispered.

She shrugged in response and carried on staring at
the map.

I wasn't giving up and I threw a few more questions
at her when Miss Wilcox turned her back to write on the
blackboard. 'Did you like the food?' 'Is your tongue still
burning from the spices?' 'My mum really likes you.'

Each time I got the shrug, which made me wonder
which part of the evening she didn't like.

In the end, I had let her think my dad was my granddad. First, because I didn't want to explain that my
parents had had an arranged marriage when Mum was
fourteen years old and that she was Dad's third wife.
Secondly, she wasn't worth the effort; I was still very
annoyed by her hurtful comment.

Julie suddenly reached across the desk for my Biro and
started scribbling over the map of Argentina. I looked up
at the teacher who was still writing on the board, then
back at Julie, not quite believing what I was seeing. Scribbling in books would earn us detention for the rest of the
year. I didn't really understand the Falklands War, apart
from Margaret Thatcher not being happy with Argentina, but I didn't expect Julie to be so patriotic.

'Are you alright?' I finally asked.

'My auntie's having a baby,' she replied, eyes down still scribbling over the contour lines. 'It's going to be brown.'

CHAPTER TWO

BREAKING AWAY

B Y THE TIME I was twelve, Mum had me fully trained in all the skills necessary to become the perfect housewife: knitting, sewing and sitting pretty. She took me to bridal evenings in the local community to watch brides having their hands and feet hennaed. She also became more attentive towards me as my body developed.

The biggest fear Muslim parents had in those days was that their daughters would bring shame upon the family. I wasn't allowed to go out on my own any more and I had to wear a headscarf and loose-fitting clothes around the house. My brothers could do what they wanted; go out at night, talk to English girls and wear Western clothes.

Dad didn't really get involved in these matters. He was busy building up the butcher's shop, working seven days a week, and never moaned. He tried to have as little as possible to do with the visitors that came to the house, who were mainly from my mum's social circle. He didn't have time for illness, people who ran to the doctor's with a headache, or signed on the dole. He enjoyed quietness, simple food and sometimes a game of chess with me on a Sunday.

By this point Mum had time on her hands. I was out at school all day and in the evenings would go to the mosque or do my homework. She asked Dad if she could help out in the shop but he didn't have anything for her to do.

However, Mum wasn't having it and decided to throw all the stereotypes of child brides and illiteracy aside to go her own way. She taught herself to read with Ladybird books, which I had to fetch from the library. During the day, she began to travel independently by randomly jumping on and off buses and getting lost for hours on end. Then she began inviting the English neighbours over for tea to practise her English. Though most of them politely declined, two did come round; they turned out to be Polish and Irish.

She admired Margaret Thatcher on telly and one day told Dad she wanted to vote at the next election. Her literary skills weren't fully polished and she needed Dad to indicate which box represented the Conservatives. Unfortunately, when she arrived at the polling station she was holding the card upside down and voted for the National Front. My dad found out by asking for a description of the ballot card, which turned out to have the tick boxes on the wrong side.

He was so annoyed he stopped speaking to her, saying enough was enough of her recent shenanigans. But she wasn't listening, she didn't care – she was on a roll.

My dad tried not to let it get to him even when she'd witter on about it during their walks in the summer evenings. Sometimes I would tag along. These were the only times I was able to see the area we lived in.

One evening we took a longer route and ended up in different part of town. We walked past a detached bungalow with a hairdressing shop attached to it with a 'For Sale' sign up. Mum stopped and stared at it for a moment then looked at Dad and suggested they buy it. My dad laughed because it looked expensive, with a big garden. They would never be able to afford the mortgage and bills on that place.

'You won't have to worry about the bills and housekeeping, I'll take care of that,' Mum said.

This made my dad laugh even louder.

It was the first time I stopped and looked at Dad

differently. Did he think she wasn't capable or was he concerned that Asian women didn't work, let alone try to run a business.

Just at that moment, an English couple came out of the house towards their car, which was parked on the drive. Mum nudged Dad to go to speak to them. He finally plucked up the courage and engaged in conversation with them about their house. They were 'polite' and excused themselves after a few minutes saying it was best he contacted the estate agents. Dad's last attempt was to ask if they would consider 'part exchange'. This made them both shake their heads and walk away.

'We live on Drayton Road,' Dad called out.

The woman stopped in her tracks and turned round. 'The Drayton Road up there?' she asked, pointing her finger in the air over her shoulder. She looked surprised, probably because it was an English area.

He nodded.

'What number?'

The couple did come round to see the house and Mum was up at the crack of dawn cleaning it. She wasn't with us any more, she was in her world, the one she had dreamt about and was now coming true. The odds were against us getting the exchange, but knowing Mum she would do anything, even if it meant selling her dowry gold.

I knew things were going to change because I understood my mother. She had grit and determination and when she wanted something, she got it. A price was agreed and an exchange was made.

Dad's biggest concern was how Mum was going to run a hairdresser's if she couldn't cut hair and had never run a business before. However, she had other plans ticking as she discovered that the only food places nearby were a bakery and a fish & chip shop. That's when she announced to Dad that she was converting the hairdressers into a kebab shop.

The kebab shop took me through my teenage years, along with the grease that clung to my hair and skin. It was a convenient set-up. The shop was attached to the house by a door leading from the back room, which had a ringer that went off when a customer came in.

I finally finished the Koran when I was fourteen; four years later than my sister, who had since passed her school exams with flying colours and was heading for university entry. My parents bought her a desk, a lamp and a comfortable chair. The bedroom was out of bounds for me in the evening while she studied.

My time after school was replaced with chopping, kneading and scrubbing, before opening the shop at 6 p.m. It shifted the dynamics between my parents and me. No longer did they see me as a child, but instead as a responsible member of the family running the house alongside them – a role usually taken by sons in our tradition. My brothers had all left home by now and were living their own lives.

Mum hired a chef from the local community. I wasn't sure if it was intentional or coincidental, but either way it raised a few eyebrows to have a man working for a woman. The chef was known to me as Uncle Hajji. Hajji wasn't his real name, nor was he my uncle, but he had done the pilgrimage journey to Mecca and therefore had the title 'Hajji'. (Hajji is for a man, Hajjah for a woman.) He lived on the other side of town with his extended family, which was so big that they were scattered over a number of terraced streets nearby. He had arranged his two daughters' marriages in Pakistan, left them there and brought back a village girl for his son to marry when he turned sixteen. His family came from a different part of Pakistan, which meant their Punjabi accent was hard for me to understand.

I didn't have many friends at the time because I wasn't allowed out, and I was working in the shop when I wasn't at school. Mum was worried that I was becoming socially isolated compared to the Pakistani girls who lived in a community. She introduced me to Hajji's many nieces. To her relief, I ended up making friends with one of them: Shazia. She was the eldest in her family and spent most school days helping her mum bring up her younger siblings. When we were in the same room as our mums we spoke fast English so they wouldn't understand. Mum was still speaking pigeon English but she was catching up. Shazia and I were the same age, but our lives were totally different.

She was engaged to her cousin as soon as her umbilical cord was cut and she was announced a girl. The cousin lived down the road from her, which I thought was weird. All the girls in Hajji's family got married young, and if it weren't for being in England, they'd have all got married as soon as their menstrual cycles kicked in. The women in his family weren't allowed to drive as it 'gave them too much independence', nor were they allowed to go out without a male escort from the family – and even then, they would have to walk 10 feet behind him, even if it was their little brother.

I never passed judgement, nor did their strict religious regime affect me, as I respected Islam as a peaceful religion.

Shazia and I got on like a house on fire. We laughed at anything and everything as if we could read each other's minds. I'd share my dramas about working with her uncle in the kebab shop and she'd gossip about everyone in the neighbourhood. I had no idea who she was talking about, couldn't keep up with all the names and sagas, but you didn't have to watch *Dallas* for entertainment when Shazia was around. My heart would sink when we said our goodbyes, knowing I would have to wait another week before I saw my best friend again, my only friend. Sundays were when my dad had time off work and the only time he could drive me over.

However, as time went on our conversations changed. More from her side than mine.

'Who are you getting married to?' Shazia asked.

'No idea.' I'd reply flatly, shrugging my shoulders.

'Cousin from Pakistan?' she continued, oblivious to my hostile body language.

'Why?' God, she's nosy, I began to think.

'You should be engaged by now…' she smiled, exposing a set of small teeth and high gums, quickly covered up by poppy red fingernails. 'It takes ages for the visa to come though.'

Shazia would wear a tight headscarf that covered all her hair, while mine hung round my neck and was only donned over my head when I served tea to guests in the living room or went to mosque. I never wanted to swap my life for hers but I did wish for the close network of aunties, cousins and nieces she had around her. Mine were all in Pakistan and my grandparents had died long before I was born, so I had no recollection of them; just a black and white photo of Dad's mum, which he kept on his bedside cabinet.

My relationship with her Uncle Hajji in the shop was distant but polite. He would give me dirty looks for no reason when I asked him a question about food orders, but it didn't bother me. I respected him as an elder member of the community and as a Hajji.

'Is this the chicken or lamb madras, Uncle?' I would ask, pointing at the foiled container he put down on the stainless steel wall between us.

Grunt.

'Uncle?'

Hand on hip, he'd toss his head the other way. Reluctantly I'd peel back the lid and check for myself.

I know he disapproved of me not wearing my headscarf the way Shazia did, and not being more subservient towards him, but I didn't care.

The dynamic between him and Mum was fascinating. She never spoke as a meek woman from as far back as I can remember, but now she made a conscious effort not to. She would march into the shop to inspect his work, speaking in a loud voice but with less drama than she used to use in the home. Less is more, as she was slowly learning from Dad. Her presence made Hajji nervous.

When the shop was quiet, I'd hear him in the back banging the pots around and making heaving noises that sounded as if he was carrying a ton of bricks on his back, and then when the shop was busy he'd flap around making dramatic arm gestures like he was some big Michelin-star chef. He'd argue with me when he'd get the order wrong, vowing I'd said chicken madras and not lamb, then blaming me for forgetting to put the chip pan on. I nicknamed him 'The Snake' because he chose his moments to tell Mum how good Shazia was to get married young before she did something to bring shame on her family, like being seen talking to a boy on the street.

The customers were a mixed bag: some were from the council estate across the road and the pub next door, others were lads in uniform from the fire station and Territorial Army barracks down the road. I would juggle my evenings between serving the customers, doing my homework and taking care of house chores. My routine was watertight and safe. I didn't mind any of it, no matter how many people asked whether I was tired or overworked.

What I did mind was guests visiting the house and having to serve tea all the time, particularly the 'auntie and uncle from Longsight'. They had recently been coming round too often for my liking. I got so sick of them that one day I deliberately broke wind as I offered a plate of Jalebi, a fried Indian sweet made from flour and syrup. Dad turned the other way and Mum looked mortified. Fortunately, the guests pretended they hadn't heard anything and carried on talking about their family in Pakistan.

I left the room in a bit of a state, worried that Mum was going to tell me off when they'd gone and then realised I'd forgotten the tray. I turned to go back inside and could hear them in full flow of conversation so stopped outside and pressed my ear to the door.

'Oh no, brother,' I heard Mum say, 'My daughter is still studying, we haven't even thought about her marriage yet.'

I knew they were talking about me. My sister's marriage had already been arranged to some chap in Pakistan and she was happy. It had been a civilised process, with agreement from both families who communicated openly. To me it was one big farce that I was not going through. I was not giving up my life to a stranger.

'What are you going to gain from letting her study, besides people talking and getting a bad name for the family?' the uncle asked with a mouthful of food.

'Maybe if she got a degree she could marry a doctor,' Mum retorted.

'Or maybe she could run away with a boy she meets at college, then which doctor will have her?' He snapped back.

The room fell quiet. I felt myself getting angry. How dare he talk to my mum like that? Also, why isn't Dad stepping in?

I heard Dad clear his throat like he'd read my

thoughts. 'Our children are brought up here and want partners brought up the same way and who speak English.'

It was the first time I had heard Dad speak up on these matters. He was a man of few words but when he spoke, he spoke sense.

'Nonsense!' the uncle interrupted. 'Are you suggesting we forget our ways? Both my son and daughter married in Pakistan and both are happy.'

They're not happy, they're scared of you, I thought.

'So what are you suggesting?' Mum asked.

'We have a nephew, who lives in Pakistan,' the uncle raised his voice a notch. 'Very educated and works in a bank.'

I imagined my parents exchanging blank looks. Firstly, this wasn't about my parents' respect, it was about getting their nephew over to England. Secondly, didn't they think my parents had nephews in their own family to choose from if they really wanted to marry me back there?

I couldn't take it any more: this was my life they were discussing. Just as I was about to barge in the shop bell rang.

Scott was stood by the shop door. He was a good-looking lad, well built, gelled-back hair, wearing a gold hoop in his left ear. He would normally come in after the pubs closed with his very pretty girlfriend or a gang of lads after a night out.

'Can I come in?' he asked, holding the door open with one foot.

'You're not allowed,' I said.

'Tell your mum I'm sorry,' he pleaded.

I looked at him and he did look sorry. A fight had erupted in the shop last night near closing time between six blokes representing different football teams for the local pubs. Hajji had hidden in the kitchen, which didn't surprise me. I recall a fist missing me by half an inch then Scott reassuring me that he would get them all out of the shop. Unfortunately, before he could finish his sentence, a punch landed on his face and he fell by Mum's favourite plant pot. That did it. Mum went round with a rolled-up newspaper and started hitting them. It was quite a sight to see six burly blokes being shooed out by her. Although Scott was part of the group, he was trying to stop the fight, but Mum decided the whole group was banned from coming in for a month.

'Hang on.' I went inside the house and pretended to speak to Mum then reappeared moments later. 'Mum said you're allowed in but it's your last chance.'

Scott leapt in, rubbing his hands in glee as he scanned the food trays in the display fridge.

'Two of them while I'm waiting, love.' He pointed at the onion bhaji tray.

I placed the bhajis in the microwave and stared anxiously at him, trying to figure out which of the two menus stuck on the wall he was looking at; the kebab or my pizza one. I'd done a deal with Mum to rent part of the fridge and start selling my own pizzas to earn my own money.

Pizzas were becoming the fashionable food. I decided to give them the authentic touch by using a spicy tomato base and toppings such as tandoori chicken pieces, curried vegetables and chilli cheese.

Scott looked across at me then back at the menus.

'Errr … go on then, I'll have a pizza,' he said, looking a little unsure. 'And can I have a kebab as well?'

I broke into a big smile, ignoring Hajji, who was stood in the back holding a tea towel in one hand watching us suspiciously. He was always suspicious when I served a bloke.

'How's business?' Scott always asked the same question.

'Really good, thanks,' I handed him the steaming bag of onion bhajis from the microwave.

'What was it before?'

'Hairdresser's,' I replied, making up his pizza. 'We converted it when we moved in.'

'Oh yeah, I remember now. Can't imagine your mum running that place … you lot don't really do much with your hair except grow it.'

'We're not allowed to cut our hair; it's a sign of femininity.'

'Yeah, but your hair looks great long, you should have it out, not tied back all the time.'

'We're not allowed.'

He smiled and took a bite of his bhaji.

I repeated the words in my head and realised how pathetic I sounded. Who said we were not allowed? Why can men in our culture cut their hair and why do Sikh men grow their hair long like women?

'So what do you make of this book that's out then?' Scott asked, changing the subject but only slightly.

'Not sure really,' I replied, knowing straight away which book he was talking about. 'I haven't read it so I can't say.'

The Satanic Verses publication had caused chaos in Manchester. It was the first time I'd realised how seriously our religion was taken by the Pakistani community, when Salman Rushdie had to go into hiding and the bearded man from Iran announced his death threat. Like many, I had never heard of the author before, but now I wanted to read the book to find out why the community was so distressed.

53

I'd put my name down for the book at the local library, but there was a long waiting list. It had sold out at most bookshops and others decided not to stock it.

Scott looked over his shoulder, like he was checking if anyone was behind. 'Bit over the top to start burning the Union Jack flag, don't you think?'

I agreed. He was referring to the imams who'd been on the news lately protesting against the book in central cities in the UK. 'You can't stop people from writing what they want ... freedom of speech and all that.'

'Well, it's like porn isn't it, love?' Scott wolfed his second bhaji.

'What?'

'If you want to read a porn mag you pick it up. It's up to you.' He suppressed laughter at my shocked expression.

'I suppose that's one way of putting it, but that's not blasphemy. Apparently the book says that Prophet Mohammed's wives were prostitutes.'

'Who knows?' he raised his hands in the air dramatically.

I lowered my eyes, wrapping up his kebab and pizza as Hajji stood behind watching us like a hawk.

'That will be £4.10, please.'

Scott handed me a fiver. 'Keep the change, love.' He winked and picked up the bag.

As soon as he left, I dashed back in the house. The Longsight guests had gone and Mum was clearing up the pots, humming some tune.

I wanted to confront Mum on the conversation I had overheard but was too angry to speak. I looked around for Dad but he had disappeared. The topic of marriage was an awkward one with Mum, let alone trying to talk it through with Dad. He was only present on these occasions because he had to be. I compared his personality to the Longsight uncle and realised how lucky I was not to have a bullish, dominating, loud-mouthed dad like a lot of girls had. Though he had stepped in when needed, I still questioned his lack of presence in my life. I wondered if he'd said the same when my sister was getting married. Perhaps he could see a difference between us. Perhaps he knew me better than I thought.

I tried reaching out to Shazia for sympathy, telling her there was no way I was going to Pakistan to get married and milk a cow every morning. Her response was to reassure me that mothers knew best. This fuelled my anger. How insensitive. Just because it suited her didn't mean it suited everyone. I began giving her the cold shoulder, even though I was to be maid of honour at her wedding the following weekend.

However, this was not my biggest concern right now. My GCSE results were coming out next week and even the best correction fluid to change the grades would not convince my dad.

Shazia's wedding took place at the local primary school with over 500 guests. Women and children packed into a small changing room with bhangra music blasting from speakers out in the corridor. Paper plates piled high with biryani soaked in ghee were passed around and the fizzy pop served in polystyrene cups was flowing. Shazia looked stunning. She wore a red sari, her face was covered in a gold net dupatta, and she had a big gold ring through her left nostril. I was dressed like a tube of glitter with Hollywood hair and Bollywood eyebrows. As maid of honour, my role was to sit beside her and collect money from the women queuing to examine the dowry gold she wore. Skilfully they scrutinised its intricate detail then lifted it away from her skin to guess its weight. Then, and only then, would they put a hand inside their bras and take out a tenner. That's when I would jolt to attention and start scribbling their names down on a jotter pad and stuffing the notes inside a big gold purse squeezed between my knees. The money would later be returned to the couple by Shazia's mum when their children got married.

The wedding was a success, a joyous occasion for everyone, but I left feeling depressed and couldn't find it inside me to be happy for her. I handed the money purse back to her mum with the excuse that I had to go home and open the shop. Something was niggling at me and I couldn't put my finger on it.

To my dismay, my GCSE results came out worse than I had expected. My parents discovered there was never a grade A on the radar. Grades were all they were concerned with so I decided to study easier subjects and took my A levels in art. It was also the convenient option because I had to juggle my studies with working in the shop every evening. The news did not go down well with my parents. Mum was horrified that I would be painting pictures of naked people and Dad couldn't understand why I wanted to be a painter/decorator.

I went on to study an art foundation course at Manchester College for one year, which I needed before applying for an art degree. My parents found it strange as they expected me to apply for a degree straight after A levels. They got suspicious that I was re-sitting A levels and using the foundation as an excuse. I, too, wasn't keen on it. It felt like my life was shortened by a year. However, if I had chosen academic subjects I'm sure my life would have been shortened by many more.

The institute, based in the city centre, was my first step into the outside world. It introduced me to a tapestry of people I had not experienced at school. The students were made up of many overseas nationalities

– Japanese, Cypriot, Swedish and American – that I'd never been exposed to before. The teachers were less rigid and were approachable, making it easier to reach out for a mentor.

Dave headed the foundation course. The first day I met him, I knew he would be my mentor. He was a man in his fifties who didn't mince his words; a similar trait to the one I saw in Mum, which I liked.

On my first few critiques, he asked what my parents thought of me studying art. There weren't many Asians studying the subject in those days, as it wasn't seen as an education, hence my parents' dismay. I stuck out like a sore thumb and he clocked on from my surname that I was Muslim. I enjoyed our friendly banter; the remarks he made about the band of gold I wore on my arm, asking if it was part of my dowry; what my brothers and sisters did and where I was in the pecking order; all the time trying to piece me together. He spotted a *Telegraph* newspaper in my portfolio once and asked if I was a Tory. I didn't understand politics much, except that the majority of art students labelled themselves as socialists. I was once asked to join a protest against some Bill going through Parliament but declined. Firstly because I didn't know enough about the Bill but also because I didn't want to be associated with a party that students signed up to just because it was seen as 'trendy'.

Dave described my kebab shop duties combined with my studies as a 77-hour weekly shift. However, I didn't see it that way. I saw it as a stable routine that gave me time every evening, between serving customers, to work on my art projects. It diverted my attention away from useless pastimes like watching television. The shop opened up a social circle of people from my local area, who provoked discussions and debates with me on matters affecting the local people and topical news issues. Dave devised my projects around my working hours in the shop and took time out to sit with me in the canteen. I was pleased to be getting the support and recognition and so I would try to stretch out our time together by offering him more coffee and cake. It got the students gossiping, but there was nothing flirtatious between us.

Boys were not on my radar as I was too busy with my work and studies, though I did make friends with one called Mark. He was a gentle giant with spiky blonde hair and a kind smile. We would meet every morning for coffee in the canteen and go to the sandwich shop together at lunchtime. One day Mark suggested we go to another place down near the canal as it served good tea.

The tea was nice but nothing special. What was more fascinating were the surroundings. There was something about the people both serving and being served at the café that I couldn't quite put my finger on; nothing odd, just different. More facial piercings, alternative clothing and tattoos.

'Have you guessed yet?' Mark ran his fingers through his hair, face flushed.

I looked at him blankly.

'You know,' his eyes flitted over to a group of young men sat at a table close by. 'I'm gay.'

A strange feeling set in in the pit of my stomach. The first time I had heard the word 'homo' was at school, bantered around like a swearword. The second time was by a Muslim girl whose family friend had died of AIDS and the community refused to attend the funeral, saying it was God's punishment. Now, here I was; my best friend telling me he was everything forbidden, dirty, and against my beliefs.

I drank my tea, finding the warm liquid comforting. I could see this was hard for him too, but for some reason he felt compelled to tell me about his personal life.

I heard a shuffling noise behind me, and then a man pulled a chair up and joined our table. He was over six foot, wore black leather trousers, a matching jacket, had a shiny head and a ring through his nostril.

'Hello, I'm Kev.' He held his hand out to me. 'I've heard a lot about you.'

I looked at Mark for help. Could this be a test from God, I wondered, pushing the most compromising scene

of them together out of my mind? I smiled back politely
and shook Kev's hand. God have mercy on you both,
I prayed silently.

The walk back to college was not full of the usual
chatter – it was awkward. I couldn't come to terms
with people who wanted to kiss someone of the same
sex. I felt deceived and tricked, as if he had hurt me
intentionally.

Thankfully, when we got back I spotted Vanessa
and broke away from Mark. Vanessa was an extremely
attractive mixed-race girl. She had been brought up in
the most deprived and gun-ridden area of Manchester
called Moss Side. Her father had left when she was a
baby and she had recently turned to religion.

'Where are you going?' I asked, as she walked past. I
knew she was on her way to church 'to get some peace',
as she put it.

I decided to tag along, which surprised her as much
as it surprised me. I had never been in a church before
nor did I know any existed in the close vicinity. When
we got there, the church was empty. We sat in the
middle row of wooden benches, staring ahead at
the stained-glass windows and a statue of Jesus hanging on a cross. It felt strange. I was used to the bright
lights of a mosque, sitting on the floor with lots of
noise around. However, as the minutes passed, I felt

the warmth of the place and began to understand what she meant by 'peace'. It gave me time to think back to Mark. I realised that the issue lay with me and not him. I was the one with the prejudice, the conditioning, and if I let it control me, I would be the one to lose. He was still my best friend, the one I wanted to share my toasted teacake with in the morning, so I had to find a way of getting over it.

*   *   *

'Why do they keep coming over?'

Mum was preparing yet another feast for the Longsight couple's arrival.

'Because we have things to talk about that unmarried girls should not be asking about.'

'Who's getting married?'

Mum was saved by the shop bell.

I put my pinny on and headed over. The living-room door was open as I walked past. Dad was inside watching the news. Iraq had just invaded Kuwait and America had gone over to help. It had kept him on an adrenalin rush. He hated America and what it stood for; a country that only took action if it benefited them, in this case – oil. The shop customers had mixed views on the situation, but most of them supported America poking its nose in and quoted from what they'd read in the papers. I didn't feel I understood enough to have a view.

Tim, one of our regular customers, was stood at the shop counter.

'Hiya, love! Can I have a kebab?' He pointed at the doner spit. 'Make it a large one with that garlic stuff and chips.'

I smiled politely. I was not in the mood for small talk tonight but he was a regular. Luckily, the noise from the electric carving knife as I sliced the doner meat made it impossible to hear what he was saying.

However, when I switched it off and turned back round, Tim had his elbows sprawled over the counter blowing smoke rings into the greasy air. I couldn't believe it, there was a 'no smoking' sign on the door before you walked in. Everyone was getting on my nerves today.

'That Madras you made the other night nearly blew my bloody head off,' he pointed the cigarette at me. 'Tell that beardy to put less chillies in next time.'

Tim was referring to Hajji, who did have a rather long beard, come to think of it. Ever since the shop opened, I had dreaded getting one of those random health and safety inspectors coming round and closing us down. If women had to tie their hair up, why didn't men put their beards in a net or something? But there was no way

I could approach Hajji on the topic; he would accuse me of blasphemy.

'I told my boss where to go the other day.' Tim was off again. 'He didn't like it but the tosser had it coming. I'll go on the dole if I have to, council can pay my rent for a change.'

I tried to think of something to say but couldn't. I kept thinking about the Longsight couple. I couldn't stand them. How dare they come round and try to take over my life! I could feel the stress going to my fingers, and then the kebab suddenly ripped and collapsed in my hand. Thankfully, Tim was looking the other way.

'Off to the pub tonight?' I asked, quickly wrapping it up.

'Yeah, wanna come?' He raised a smile.

I ignored his comment and gave him the silent treatment, which usually worked.

'So, what've you been up to, love?' he asked.

It did.

'I went to a wedding.' Mum knew so many people in our community that she was invited to weddings most weekends and she dragged me along to showcase me in front of women who had eligible sons and nephews.

'One of your lot?' Tim let out a smoker's cough, which sounded disgusting mixed with the phlegm at the back of his throat. 'Is that what you'll be having?'

He was pushing all the right buttons, fishing for a big debate on what he'd read in the tabloid papers about forced marriage. I hated the ignorance of some English people round here.

Tim lit another cigarette and gazed into space. 'If it was up to my mum I'd end up with some specky, four-eyed librarian.'

What's wrong with that? I wanted to say, but instead scurried into the kitchen.

Beardy reappeared from prayers and started banging the spoons around in the back. Recently we were getting under each other's feet and it was always I who had to apologise. His response was to tut dramatically and turn his head away.

I watched him fret over the bubbling pans on the cooker. His eyes were red from peeling a sack of onions earlier and his white coat was stained at the hips from shocking red tandoori paste. This marriage thing was getting me down and I knew this 'snake' was fuelling my mother. I wanted to grab his prayer cap off his head and kick him up his bum. Instead, I gave him Tim's order of chips and headed inside the house.

This time I didn't stop at the door to listen, but barged in. I wanted to know what was going on. The room fell silent. All four of them, my parents and the Longsight couple, were huddled around the coffee table staring up at me.

'I just wanted to check if you wanted more tea,' I said, trying to figure out why the auntie was clutching her handbag so tight.

Mum shook her head.

Purposely, I left the door slightly ajar when I walked out so that I could peer inside between the nick.

They all turned back into one another again.

'So, yes … he's from the same caste, you have no worries,' the auntie reassured Mum.

That surprised me. I hadn't realised Pakistanis had castes. I'd thought they only existed in India. Now that I thought about it, however, Pakistan was originally part of India.

'When are we going to get to see a picture of him?' Mum sipped her tea, trying to remain cool and in control by leaning back and crossing her legs.

'You can see him now.' The auntie put a hand in her handbag and rummaged for what seemed like ages and then finally pulled out a notebook. She flicked through the pages until a passport photo dropped out.

My heart pounded as I watched Mum take the photo from her, a little too quickly, and study it. The room was so quiet I could hear the cars outside on the road through the double-glazed window.

'He's very handsome,' Mum finally said, and passed it onto Dad.

Dad stared at it for a lot longer, making the uncle light another cigarette straight after finishing one. Dad didn't comment and passed it back to the auntie.

'What do you think, brother?' she asked my dad with a nervous laugh.

'He looks a lot younger than twenty,' Dad replied flatly.

'It was taken a few years ago when he was a student … but he hasn't changed much.'

'Yes,' Mum agreed quickly. 'Children don't change.'

I didn't believe any of it. It was one of two things: either he was pretending to be older, or he was much older and they were showing a college photo to hide his age.

I thought back to my recent critique with Dave at college, when he said I'd probably be staying in Manchester to do my degree. The thought hadn't occurred to me as we were still a few weeks away from applying for degree places.

'Why do you think that?' I had asked.

'Well, who's going to look after the shop?'

His words turned over and over in my head; the more I thought about it the more I realised this place wasn't my future. I didn't want to look back in a few years' time and wished I'd done something different. However, I was also torn with the dilemma of hurting my parents and going against their will. The struggle became bigger in my head.

There were two ways to do it; either I leave without saying a word and put my parents through hell or, for the same result, I face the music.

But first I needed to secure a place somewhere. This was my life and my choice.

I decided to study at Bristol as it had a good art department and was close to Bath, which I'd heard was beautiful.

It was only once I had been accepted at Bristol that I realised I was about to make a drastic departure from the world I'd been brought up in. I made my first attempt of breaking the news to Mum, which went down like a lead balloon. I used the excuse that the subject I wanted to study wasn't available in Manchester. 'Pick another,' she replied.

For some reason I hadn't thought she would respond so logically. I pursued this in front of Dad. His reaction was just to sit on the sofa, flicking his eyes between Mum and me as we stood above him arguing. Every so often Mum would spin round to him for a reaction, but he wasn't giving anything away. It was annoying as I expected more reaction from him. I expected him to say *something* at least. My brothers didn't have to go through this, so why did I? Why did boys have different rules?

The second attempt was on a Tuesday evening when the shop was quiet and Mum and I were both sat at the table in the back room. Dad sat on the armchair reading the *Daily Jang* newspaper.

I was doing an art project on my drawing board, smudging the pastel colours with my thumb. Mum was picking small stones out of a bowl of dry lentils.

'Why can't I study away?' I finally said, rubbing an invisible line out on my drawing.

'Because girls don't leave home before marriage,' Mum replied, matter of fact. 'We don't want you getting into bad company.'

'I could be doing that now,' I replied. 'You don't know what I get up to when I say I'm going to college all day. But I'm not. There's more to life than boys.' It came out before I could stop myself. I had never spoken like this before.

The brushing noise of her fingers trailing through the lentils stopped. I held my breath, preparing for a telling off, only to be faced with a wall of silence. My eyes flickered up and I noticed she was lost for words. I wasn't sure if this was because of my sudden upfront behaviour or by the words spoken. Either way, it worked, something happened. Dad looked up from his paper. Tears sprang to my eyes. I didn't want either of them to see this weak side of me. Head down, I ran into the bathroom. I blew my nose as quietly as possible so they wouldn't hear, and prayed the shop bell wouldn't ring before the puffiness around my eyes reduced. It felt like I had been grieving for a life I'd lost before it had begun. I just couldn't imagine a life like my sister's or Shazia's. I didn't see myself as special or better, it just wasn't me.

Finally, I came out of the bathroom and saw my dad stood outside looking down at me.

Did he hear my sniffling? Was he going to tell me off for speaking to Mum in that way?

'I'm sorry I spoke to…'

I noticed he was looking at me in a peculiar way, almost straight through me.

'You've always been self-sufficient. The shop will look after itself.'

It was like decrypting some World War Two code. At least with Mum she said what she thought.

'Dad, I promise I will call every night, come home every weekend…'

He opened his arms and embraced me with the biggest hug I'd had in a long time.

Over the following few days the conversations between Mum and I were minimal. In the shop, I just called out the curry orders to her and Hajji and carried on serving at the front. If the order went wrong, we did not argue about it like we normally did, I just re-did it.

It came round to another Friday evening and the shop

was chocka after the pubs closed, with people trying to get their orders in before we shut at 12 p.m. Mum handed me an order of lamb madras and Pillai rice she had prepared.

'You can go!' she shouted over the noise.

'What?' I shouted back, thinking she was saying something about the order.

'Bristol.' She touched my fingers as I took the foiled containers from her. 'You can go.'

I was up all night not quite believing what Mum had said. Part of me thought I'd dreamt it and part feared she might change her mind.

The next morning I was up early and headed into college to tell Dave the good news. The canteen was surprisingly busy for that time of the year and I joined a table of six students trying to listen into their conversation. Someone was being congratulated for being accepted to Central Saint Martins.

I leaned over and looked down the table. 'Where?'

'Central Saint Martins in London … it's one of the best art colleges.'

I was dumbstruck. I had never heard of the place, but if I had, I would have applied there instead. I suddenly felt this ball of adrenalin build up inside me. I felt like I'd been short-changed in some warped way. Just then, Dave walked in and headed over to the sandwich bar.

'Dave.' I sped up to him as he inspected a cheese roll wrapped in cling film. 'I've changed my mind; I want to go to Saint Martins.'

Dave looked bemused, not knowing where this had come from, then threw me a sympathetic smile. 'I think you have enough things to deal with … have you told your parents you're leaving?'

My mind wasn't on my parents any more; Bristol or London – it was the same story to them.

'You'll love it in Bristol,' he continued, putting the sandwich back down and walking over to the drinks machine. 'Besides, what makes you think you're good enough to get into Saint Martins?'

That was the best thing Dave could have ever said to me. That night I lay awake and couldn't get his words out of my head. He was someone I respected. Did he really think I wasn't good enough to get in? The next morning I found myself in a phone box down the road from the house calling up Central Saint Martins.

The lady on the other end of the telephone was firm, telling me all the places were full this year but that I could come and see the degree show with a view to applying the following year. That evening I told Mum I was attending an art exhibition and might be a bit late home, but would prepare the salad bowls for the shop in the morning before going to college. I'd saved up enough money from the pizzas sold in the shop to buy a travel ticket.

With my big portfolio tucked under an armpit, I caught the train to London. I'd never been to the big city and got lost on the underground, finally rising up in the lift to ground level at Covent Garden, where the graphics building was then located on Long Acre. The entrance of the college was deserted. At the top of the stairs, I was faced with four doors with no labels. I spun round, not knowing which one to knock, then a man came out of one. He had a stocky build, was wearing an eccentric floral shirt, and had the most amazing moustache that curled up at each end.

'Yes, can I help?' He bent forward, sticking one ear inches away from my face.

Perhaps he thinks I have a quiet voice, I thought. I spoke extra loud, asking if I could see a first-year tutor because I wanted to apply to come this summer. The man repeated word-for-word what the woman on the phone had told me.

'But I've travelled three hours on the train.' I persisted. 'Can they not spare ten minutes, please?'

He could see the desperation on my face. He went quiet for a moment then asked me to wait there and disappeared through one of the doors.

I stood still and gathered my thoughts, not quite

believing I was here. Only yesterday I was feeling ecstatic about Mum letting me go to Bristol. A part of me waited for the doubt to kick in, but it didn't. This was where I wanted to be and I wasn't leaving until I gave it my best shot.

The man suddenly came out of a different door and waved me in. I followed him inside where three tutors were sat having a drink. They were probably in the middle of enjoying their end-of-year get-together and I was disturbing them, I thought guiltily.

Quickly, I opened my portfolio and ran through my work. (I had a two o'clock train to catch, which would get me back in time to open the shop.) The interview was mainly made up of questions on why I'd come here today. I told them the truth: from the moment that I'd heard Saint Martins being mentioned just twenty-four hours ago in my college canteen, to getting on the train this morning and being here. They flicked through my pieces of work then said I would get a letter from them in the morning.

I nodded my head, my only concern now being catching the train back to Manchester.

That night I tossed and turned in bed at the day's events, then rose early and hovered around the front door of the house, waiting for the postman. Yesterday's events felt surreal now. Only the letter would tell me if it had really happened.

The post eventually fell on the mat.

I stared at the white envelope addressed to me with a Central Saint Martins stamp on the front.

I opened it and smiled uncontrollably as I read the words: Accepted at the college this September.

CHAPTER THREE

THE BIG CITY

LEFT HOME with two carrier bags and a set of tasbih prayer beads. Perhaps it was out of habit or the ritual I was brought up with from my mosque days, but somehow my day didn't feel right without repeating a line from the Koran over each of the hundred beads and saying a prayer.

Waking up for the first time in the Tooting Broadway halls of residence felt strange. I'd never been away from home before, not even on sleepovers as a kid. I couldn't hear my mum calling from the kitchen; I didn't have to think about cutting the salad before the shop opened, or cooking Dad's dinner.

Judging from the corridor noise of students on their way to college, I knew I had overslept.

I decided to wear a pink flowery top, velvet jacket, and maroon lipstick, with a range of bright eyeshadow colours making my eyes look like butterflies on my first day of college. Most of my clothes were bright and silky with bold flowers. I still wore my gold bangles that weighed heavy, made marks on my wrist and jingled all the time. I also wore a gold necklace with red and green stones and dangly Indian-style earrings.

The first thing that struck me as I walked down Tooting High Street was the number of Afro-Caribbeans. I'd never seen so many in my life.

The train station was crowded by my standards, and after talking to the ticket officer I bought a weekly travel pass and headed down the escalator for the train.

People on the train didn't speak and the whole carriage was silent – very strange. I sat next to a woman and started talking. She looked down at her bags, making sure they were still there, and then got off at the next stop. How weird, I thought, thinking back to my bus journeys in Manchester where everyone talked. Never mind, once they see me on the train a few times we will get chatting. For some reason, I assumed I would see the same people on the train in the same carriage the next day, as I did on the bus in Manchester.

When I arrived at college I got another surprise: the students didn't look at all as I expected. Less conventional than Manchester, they didn't seem to wear high-street fashion. Instead, they wore weird clothes, listened to strange music, and a lot of them smoked. Girls looked unfeminine with their scruffy jeans and baggy jumpers, and wearing no make-up, not even eyeliner. I wondered what they thought of me in my conventional jeans and flat, comfortable shoes.

Living at the halls became an issue. I longed to cook chapattis and hot curry, which the kitchen didn't facilitate. Students would get drunk, be sick, then spend their weekend in bed. Perhaps they took this freedom and independence for granted, but to me it was a waste of life.

Now I didn't have the kebab shop in the evenings and weekends, I was going mad with boredom. I tried to find a job in a fashionable clothes shop in Covent Garden but they didn't seem impressed with my kebab shop CV. Working in another kebab shop would be like taking a step back.

I moved out of the halls after the first term into a bedsit in Wood Green. It was a dreary place, but felt more like living in society than the isolated student hub of the halls. I couldn't stand being surrounded by students any more. I wanted to meet different people. I felt removed from life.

The fear of being financially deprived always played

at the back of my mind. I remember the jumble-sale clothes Mum made me wear to school, and sometimes having to leave home in the morning without breakfast because there was no food in the fridge. Thankfully, in those days the government supplied milk for kids at schools. Secondary school was worse, when my parents started up their businesses. I had to wear the same uniform every year, while others, whose parents didn't work, received government allowances for new ones each year. I remember once being laughed at by a girl because I had a big hole in my shoe – my parents couldn't afford new ones.

In the first year of college, we were left to experiment freely on art projects to bring out our individual styles. Mine was bright colours. It didn't matter what the brief was or materials supplied, I just went for bright colours. The teachers concluded it was because of my background, no matter how much I insisted it was my personal style.

A few months in, I learnt how prestigious the art college was and how many famous people had previously attended. Most of the students in my year either had parents who were big in the art world or came from wealthy overseas families. I tried not to let it get to me, but it was difficult to connect with people who had no idea what it was like to live on a budget in a bedsit and not be able to discuss art careers with their family.

However, the teachers seemed to notice. Andrew, the head of our year, was a handsome, softly spoken man who reminded me of my dad in his younger years. He told me I had a disadvantaged background compared to most students and if I wanted to stay ahead, I would have to learn the new Apple computer programmes that had just come in. It was a new technology and everyone was in the same boat. The college had just set up a computer room with a handful of these new computers. As expected, they were in high demand and difficult to get on.

Andrew suggested I talk to Robert, the man with the amazing curling moustache, who I had met at my interview, to see if I could get onto the computer classes he ran outside college hours. Finally, I had found something to replace the kebab shop. I missed being busy. I would leave the bedsit at 6 a.m. to attend the earlybird classes, then stay behind after college and go in at the weekends.

It also brought me closer to the teachers, who drew me into interesting debates, the biggest one being about religion. All my life I had thought Jesus was Muslim because he is mentioned in the Koran, until one day Andrew told me he was Jewish. It left me stunned for days. Does this mean Islam accepts the Jewish religion? I asked myself. If so, why do we have separate books, and why wasn't any of this explained to me at the mosque? I remembered the religious wars between Muslims, Christians and Jews, when I was growing up: the poisonous enmity between Catholics and Protestants during the IRA bombings; the Sunnis' and Shiites' seven-year war in Iran and Iraq. I wanted to find out about these other religions and began with the Brompton Oratory Church. It was magical. I discovered that names mentioned in the Bible, like Abraham, Isaac and Sarah, were also in the Koran. The best part was, when I bought an English translation of the Koran, half the stories were the same as those in the Bible. I began to wonder, who copied who?

The experience set me off on a journey visiting synagogues, Hindu temples, Buddhist retreats and even a couple of cult groups to get a handle on how religion became so powerful that it made people kill one another. I never got the answer, but throughout this journey I recited my prayers from the Koran. Islam was my faith and always would be, though I now had to accept Jesus was not Muslim, I also didn't believe he was Jewish or Christian, but perhaps a mixture of all three.

Towards the end of the year, Robert offered me a place on the summer computing course. I hesitated, as

I had a limited grant, which meant that I couldn't afford to stay in London during the holidays. It had been playing on my mind for some time and I had done another round of shop interviews but hadn't got anywhere.

I was taken aback when Andrew offered me his home to stay in because he was off to France.

The house was situated in south London on a leafy street. I arrived with a carrier bag of clothes. Andrew handed me a set of keys and showed me around. I left the bag in the main bedroom, where he'd laid clean sheets on the bed, then followed him downstairs, all the time looking out for his wife. We sat at the kitchen table having a cup of tea, running through how the heating and water worked, when I heard the front door close. It's her, I thought, imagining Andrew's wife to be a pretty blonde, perhaps French.

A man entered and touched Andrew affectionately on the shoulder. My mind went to their bed upstairs, the one I would be sleeping in, and I began to panic. 'You're gay!' I screamed inside. I wanted to find an excuse to leave but couldn't think of one. Then I stopped myself, suddenly feeling ashamed. Neither Andrew nor his partner was judging me for being Pakistani like most of the people I grew up with had. Instead, Andrew had welcomed me with open arms and had kindly offered me his home. He didn't have to do this, nor did he have to mentor me the way he had. I thought back to Mark's partner and how insulted he had looked at my hostility. I had no right to judge what people did in their personal lives. I smiled at the man, then shook his hand and planted a big kiss on his cheek.

Towards the end of the summer break, I called up loads of design houses for work experience and finally got a place at a magazine publisher based in the city. The work was rewarding and the art director allowed me to use the computers, which had the latest graphic programs installed, so I could learn how to use them.

The offices had a 24-hour security guard, who the art director introduced me to. She said I could go into the offices in the evenings and at weekends to use her computer to practise. Later she commissioned me to do a computer illustration for one of the magazines and I was paid a whopping £40. What was more satisfying than the money, though, was seeing my name in print. By the end of the summer, I had learnt three new programmes and had been offered regular illustration work for a magazine. I moved back to my bedsit just before college began again. I now had money in the bank and felt like I was finally settling into the city.

My visits home continued. Hajji was also doing my job now, serving at the front of the shop. He didn't look pleased about it and totally blanked me when I'd go in and say hello. The last time we'd worked together before I left, I had supervised him putting an order together, which included a tandoori chicken he forgot to take out of the microwave, so the customer went home with an empty box ... of course, I got the blame.

My sister was now happily married and had moved away, so it was just me at home with Mum and Dad. I tried to contact Shazia a few times to tell her I was back, but each time her mother-in-law answered and said she was 'busy'. It was annoying, but at the same time, I felt relieved. My life had changed so much I wasn't sure we would have much to talk about any more.

Mum continued to pursue me on the marriage front. It was draining. I wasn't going to get married. There were two ways I could approach this: either I kept fighting this losing battle, or, for the sake of sanity, I could go along with it and stretch the process out with excuses.

'I've been thinking,' she said, flicking through the TV channels. 'We could try to get you married to someone here.' It was said like she was doing me a favour. 'A woman is not happy without a man in her life,' she offered wisely. 'Without a husband she is not a woman.'

Perhaps marriage is something people do to keep loneliness at bay, I wanted to say; a distraction in their lives.

Mum was never good at silences. She reached for her handbag and brought out a wad of papers. At first, I thought it was paperwork for the shop and felt a trickle of relief that the conversation had moved on.

'I spoke to a marriage bureau and they gave me these forms to fill out,' she said, holding them out to me.

I took the papers, which looked like a job application, and flicked through. It mentioned caste.

'What caste are we, Mum?'

'Ah.' Mum switched the television off and sat up. 'It's best we put my family caste down as it's higher than your father's.'

I was surprised Mum had been allowed to marry into a lower caste. Then I thought of Dad's credentials: army man, educated and invited to England by the British government for his service in India.

I scanned through the rest of the form, and then a cheeky thought crossed my mind.

'Most of it is general information about me,' I said, ticking the boxes referring to me as divorced, with three children, aged forty-six. I handed it back and waited for the guilt to kick in – but nothing happened. Instead, I felt satisfied that I had implemented the first stage of my plan to string this process out as much as possible.

* * *

The second year at college was more structured, but with less handholding. We were left to do our own projects and only came together for briefings or to show our work. The studios were empty most of the day but I would go in to keep my routine. I hardly saw the teachers, but one day as I was sat in the deserted studio the head teacher spotted me and came over. He was a very quiet man with grey hair and round glasses. He looked like Harry Potter but forty years on.

'Adi,' he said, walking towards me. 'Is it Adi or Abi?'

I didn't take offence as a lot of people got my name wrong; Adi, Abi … I'd even been called 'Asda' once.

'I got a call from a local publisher who is looking for someone to do their show cards,' he announced.

I didn't know what show cards were but agreed to go and see them about the job. The office was open plan with lots of people talking on the phone or on computers. It had a big, posh reception area, security guards and cameras. It was all very daunting but I tried not to show my nerves.

There wasn't much of an interview. They asked my name and who had sent me and then showed me the job and told me what I'd be paid. There wasn't much to making up show cards apart from sticking book jackets onto boards to be shipped off to bookshops to promote a new book.

The job was taking up most of my time outside college, though I did squeeze in the odd illustration for the magazine.

Soon after, my boss moved to a different publisher and offered me more work there. I couldn't turn it down, not after waiting so long to fill up my time.

My daily routine expanded to working at one publisher in the morning until 8.30 a.m., spending the rest of the day at college, and then working evenings at the other publisher's until midnight.

Towards the end of my second year, I began to wonder how I was going to spend my second summer in London. The work routine was set around my college time and I needed something to fill in the gaps during the holidays. I was sat in the computer room mulling it over when I overheard a postgrad student talk about a job they had just got with a design house in Soho. I called them up and got an interview. They thought I was also postgraduate and told me the pay was £12 an hour. My jaw dropped at the thought of earning almost £100 a day... that was how much my dad got a week. I finished the summer job with a list of contacts that I used to get freelance work during my final year, and by the time I left college I had set myself up as a self-employed designer.

It felt great but I soon realised my employment years

were going to be more challenging than those spent at college. I sensed judgement being passed by my colleagues because of my accent, but when they discovered I had attended Central Saint Martins they changed their tune. I detested this stereotyping and wondered how they would react if I told them I had attended one of the roughest state schools in Manchester.

It didn't bother me – if anything, it fired me to succeed. My mindset changed: I took a streamlined approach to life, choosing not to get involved with colleagues' moaning and office politics. I became more selective about the people I socialised with, avoiding those who drained their energy on useless twitter about relationships, family conflicts and people at work. My focus was to save enough money to buy my own place.

When I was twenty-four years old, I bought my first flat. People at work thought my parents had given me the money, people who knew me laughed when I told them.

I'd been out of college for a few years by this point. The money kept coming in but the work became repetitive. I felt I'd reached a plateau and couldn't see where I was going next. I reached out to my old teacher, Andrew, who urged me to stay ahead of the game and consider developing my CV if I wanted to step into something new.

He talked about a new Master's degree that focused

on converging technologies and the emerging digital age of the internet. It was part time so I could keep working and earning a living. It was now the mid-1990s and the internet was simmering in the background.

I finished the degree in the late '90s, just as the internet boom kicked off. The *FT* had started a section on 'Internet & Technology', which I read on a regular basis. One morning an article about an internet start-up in the States, which focused on marketing rather than the technology, caught my eye.

I finalised a business plan, closely related to internet marketing technology I'd read about in the newspaper, to set up my own company and went to a few banks for a loan. All the banks turned me down. Disheartening as it was, I decided to get myself set up from my bedroom. It took many long and lonely months of blagging to build up enough corporate clients to receive seed capital and office space. What surprised me most was when I'd meet clients and they would ask me if Mr Ahmed was attending. I would reply, 'I am Miss Ahmed,' then sit down.

Throughout all of this my parents knew nothing about my internet business, Master's degree or property interests. They still thought I was a painter. I continued to fob Mum off by saying I had a temporary job and would return home afterwards. I knew this would

never happen. London gave me a life that made returning home impossible. It gave me independence, a place
to build my career, and opportunities to meet a tapestry
of interesting people. The only downside was leading a
double life with my parents. It made me feel both guilty
and confused, but it was the price I had to pay.

Everything was ticking along nicely and my life was
full and very busy. Soon, however, I became restless.

One day I shared my concerns with an old friend
whom I'd met at a publishing house where I was
working previously. She jokingly suggested I join the
Territorial Army.

'What's that?' I asked.

CHAPTER FOUR

FEMALE SELECTION

I DIDN'T KNOW the army had a part-time unit or that they allowed women to join. I laughed at the idea. This world was so alien to me. More importantly, I couldn't just walk away from my company and the responsibilities that went along with it. However, a part-time version could work. I remembered seeing *The Krypton Factor* on TV when I was a kid and the assault course in operation at some army barracks, and this gave me a vision of the Territorial Army as a fun recreation hobby I could do on the side while running the company.

However, there was also something intriguing about entering into another, new world, yet somehow familiar because of my father's background.

I rang the TA general enquiries line and ordered an information pack. The brochure had a list of all the units the army encompassed. They all looked interesting but my eye kept going back to the SAS blurb. It was described as the elite force. If I was going to go for it, I was going for the best, just as I had with Central Saint Martins.

I had no idea what 'SAS' stood for, though I did remember a vague clip of the Libyan Embassy siege being televised when I was a kid.

The next day I dialled the number provided for the unit; after being put on hold for a couple of minutes, I was transferred to someone who gave me a date and time to go in and see an officer at the Chelsea Barracks in London. I was surprised that they didn't ask about my qualifications or skillset – not even why I wanted to join.

I didn't tell my family I had an interview nor did I have any plans to; they didn't need to know everything I was doing in London. I did tell my friend that I had contacted the army, at her suggestion, and got an interview with the SAS. She laughed and told me that I had obviously made a mistake and that it must be some other unit that I was going to see. I let it go and never mentioned it again.

*   *   *

'Name?'

'Azi ... Azi Ahmed.'

I smiled nervously at the security officer sat in a Portakabin guarding the barracks' gates. He picked up the phone and punched four numbers, his eyes locked into mine as he waited for an answer.

My long hair was flying everywhere, the strands over my face catching on my pink lip gloss. I glanced over my shoulder onto the King's Road; it was dark, wet and busy with traffic.

I had no idea what roles were available and had brought a copy of my CV detailing my work and qualifications. I also put down that I enjoyed going to the gym because I wanted to do the physical army training as well as office-based work.

'Ah, good evening. I have a Miss Ahmed here to see you.' The security officer was now speaking down the phone. 'Yes, no problem ... OK ... yes ... will do.'

He put the phone down, leaned out of the Portakabin and pointed inside the barracks.

'OK ... straight across, through the gates, second right, to the end, up the first set of stairs and someone will meet you there.'

For some reason I thought I'd be taken there by him or someone would come down and take me up as I'd experienced in previous interviews. I picked up my handbag from the small ledge between us and made my way across the blackened courtyard, wide eyed.

Frantically I repeated the directions in my head. What gates? I couldn't see any and began to panic, thinking I should go back and ask the security guard if he could come with me. The place was so quiet I could hear my stilettos clicking against the concrete. A cold wind blew up my trouser leg and I wished I'd put a jumper beneath my jacket, as my thermal vest wasn't working.

Through sheer luck I found the gates the security guard was talking about and headed up. A man dressed in khaki uniform with black boots and a sandy beret was waiting. He was tall and ginger. I stopped and stared up at him. It was the first time I had seen anyone wearing army uniform in real life and it made him look intimidating, especially with no smile.

'Miss Ahmed?' he asked, giving me the once over.

I nodded, putting my hand out to him to shake.

'I'll take you up,' he said, ignoring my hand and punching a combination into the metal keypad behind, to release a gate. I followed him inside and down the dimly lit corridor, trying to keep up with his fast pace.

I tried to make conversation with him about the cold weather outside but his boots squeaked loudly on the polished parquet flooring making it awkward. It was a strange atmosphere. It felt like I had stepped into a different world, a world I didn't belong to, but for some reason I'd decided to be here. It made me both scared and excited.

Ginger stopped abruptly outside one of the many office doors. I skidded behind, missing him by a couple of inches.

He knocked twice on the door.

'Come in,' a voice called from inside.

Ginger opened the door and let me go through. The room looked like a normal office; a few framed certificates on the wall and a large desk in the middle where an officer sat busily scribbling away. His face resembled that of a squirrel: high cheekbones, a pointy jaw line, with short spiked hair on top of his head.

His eyes flicked to a chair across from him. 'Take a seat.'

I bounced into the room and looked round at Ginger, expecting him to come in or at least say something, but instead he closed the door and disappeared. What was it with this place? Nobody smiled! Why all the seriousness? Normally when I went for interviews, there was lots of small talk before and after. Here they hadn't even offered me a glass of water.

I did as I was told, feeling my mouth dry up as I put my handbag down on the floor and crossed my legs.

He made me wait some time before putting his pen

down, shuffling the papers to one side and leaning back in his chair, hands behind head. 'So, you want to join the unit?'

I thought back to my friend's comment about mistaking the unit and nodded. 'The SAS … yes.'

'Pardon?'

'Sorry … yes, please.' I could feel a tingling above my lips but didn't dare wipe the sweat away.

'Which unit have you come from?'

I stared at him blankly.

What did he mean by this? My CV didn't say anything about units, just the design companies I'd worked for and details of my paintings. Perhaps I should have researched the SAS before coming here, I thought, so I could understand his question, but then again I didn't research Central Saint Martins before I rocked up.

'I haven't come from another unit,' I finally said, then started telling him the story about my friend suggesting I join up, and that I was considering doing the job full time in the future if it was enjoyable.

He watched me with a poker face, which only made me talk faster and I probably sounded like I was speaking gibberish.

'Miss Ahmed,' he interjected with a bored expression. 'You need basic military training at one of the other units for a few years, followed by officer training.' He took a long pause. 'Then, if you're still interested, we can sit down and have another chat.'

I stared at him. This wasn't how I imagined the interview going. I didn't know how to respond. I had no idea what he expected, nor did he ask anything about me, so there wasn't much to discuss. A part of me wanted to reach into my handbag and bring out my CV, but I thought it best to keep up the verbal interaction. 'Isn't there…'

He shook his head before I finished. 'It doesn't work like that round here.'

Why the hell did you get me to come here tonight then? I thought angrily. Was this some sort of charade, or a complete misunderstanding? I wasn't asked about my military experience on the phone, nor was it explained to me that I needed to be at officer level to enter. How the hell could they make a mistake like that? How many Ahmeds were there in this place? I thought.

A loud knock on the door interrupted my laser-beam stare at him. A man wearing smart uniform, with dark, slicked-back hair walked in. 'John, do you have the file for the overseas training next year?' he spoke in a very posh accent.

I didn't bother looking around. I was still cross with the officer's behaviour. I'd never been treated in this cold manner at an interview before. Why was he being so horrible to me? Or was he just being 'army-like'?

The officer jumped up from his chair and stood to attention, then leaned to one side of his desk and began sieving through a pile of files.

'Yes, sir, right here.' The officer handed the man a blue file and their eyes locked for a moment. 'This is Ahmed.' The officer introduced. 'Ahmed – the colonel.'

The colonel! I sprang to my feet, scraping the chair leg loudly against the floor and quickly offering my hand. He was very tall, well over six feet.

'Ahmed's come to find out more about the unit, sir. We've been discussing the possibility of officer training then reviewing her position at a later date.'

The colonel smiled at me and started asking me questions about what I did for a living.

By this time I'd clocked on that they were clearly not interested in my paintings and internet company and so I needed another tactic. Then it came to me and I told him about Dad's time in the British Indian Army. I prayed the colonel wouldn't ask any difficult questions like which unit my father was in or which rank he had held. I had no idea because he had never talked about it. Luckily, the colonel just listened then tucked the file under his arm and left the room.

I didn't know what he had made of it. It was a weak attempt and perhaps not relevant but I gave it my best. It suddenly dawned on me that I'd only thought about

Dad's army life as I stood in front of the colonel and wondered why I hadn't thought about putting it on my CV, which was still sitting in my handbag.

I sat back down and looked across at the officer, who was now scribbling something down.

'I suggest your first point of contact is general enquiries,' he said, handing me a piece of paper. 'They will take it from there.'

I glanced at the number, which was the same one I'd called to order the brochure, then back at him. He was now busy sifting through some files.

A part of me wanted to say something, but I didn't know what. He'd made up his mind and blocked every channel of conversation I could attempt. I was really cheesed off and felt like a prat sitting there.

'Thank you,' I said, putting my hand out to him to shake, but he was so engrossed in those damn files he didn't notice, so I retracted and left the room.

Ginger was waiting outside and led me out of the building to the Portakabin by the main gates. Not a word passed between us. However, this time I didn't care and just wanted to get out of the place.

'Goodnight,' the security officer said as I passed.

I smiled at him, a bit embarrassed that he was seeing me again so quickly. I checked my watch: fifteen minutes, that's all it took, and ten of those involved getting in and out of the building. It was the worst interview I'd ever had. But now, having met the colonel, it felt like the place I most wanted to be. It had 'challenge' written all over it.

As soon as I got out, my phone rang and it was Mum, which was even more depressing. She wanted me to come home that weekend. I wondered how she would react if I told her I wanted to join the army. Though it would be difficult to gauge her reaction, I imagined she would be shocked and very upset. It was rare to hear about Pakistani men being in the British Army let alone a Pakistani girl.

Mum then dropped the bombshell that she and Dad were going on hajj and wanted me to go with them. I tried to remain calm as she prattled on about the 'pink' and 'blue' jobs; Mum organising the suitcases and Dad meeting the local imam to organise the flights. In our tradition if someone invites you to hajj it cannot be turned down unless it's a matter of life and death.

I asked if Dad was there. She went quiet for a second. I'd never asked to speak to him on the phone before.

'No.' There was surprise in her voice. 'What do you want to speak to him about?'

I didn't reply. I was interested to know about his time in the army, at least his role and rank.

That night I tossed and turned in bed, not about my

parents' spiritual journey but about the army interview. I felt sheer disappointment with myself, and I wished I could go back in time and change my approach or have said something different.

I couldn't get the officer out of my head: his glazed eyes, neglecting to shake my hand, and all-round dismissive aura. All these things collectively made me feel like a failure. Nevertheless, I had to let it go, I told myself bleakly.

It took a few days to blank out the experience and just when I thought I'd got it out of my system, it all came flooding back one evening when I was working late in the office. I got a phone call from the barracks asking me to come in that same evening.

The journey back down to the barracks was just as cold and dark as the last. I was anxious to get there and get on with the job they had lined up for me. I forgot to take my CV because I was in a hurry to get out of the office. I also didn't have time to check up on the ranks. I was seeing a captain tonight and had no idea where he stood in the rankings as opposed to an officer; nor had I foung out what SAS stood for.

The security officer in the Portakabin was different to the one last week but he was wearing an identical dark pullover with white collars sticking out. He stared at me, bemused, as I approached him.

'Hello,' I said with a smile, feeling more upbeat. 'I've come to see Captain Wood.' A gust of wind blew from behind, making the lapel of my coat flap over my cheek. I'd tied my hair back in a ponytail this time and applied clear lip gloss.

The security officer continued to stare at me for a moment then picked up the phone and punched some numbers in. He did not smile, but I was getting used to that.

Someone answered; I could tell because he turned his back to me and began talking down the phone. I couldn't hear what was being said because of the traffic behind, but his shiny head nodded a few times and then he turned back and looked at me.

'Did you come to see someone here a few weeks ago?' he asked.

'Last week,' I corrected. 'Is it in the same building?'

He shook his head and gave me another set of directions and handed me a visitor ID badge.

'Room 342, someone will meet you up there.'

I pinned the badge onto my coat and entered the barracks.

The courtyard was empty, but this time it was lit by floodlights so I could see the surroundings more; there were two old brick buildings stood on either side of the courtyard about four floors high. The first set of windows was six feet off the ground so I couldn't see inside, and there were a couple of large army vehicles parked at the far end.

The directions didn't seem so complicated this time and I arrived at the office within minutes.

I knocked twice and entered.

'You must be Ahmed.' Captain Wood was sat behind a desk staring at a computer screen. He didn't look at all as I expected; late fifties with a mole on his left cheek, wearing very large glasses that almost filled his face.

He signalled for me to sit in the chair opposite him. I did so and patiently waited for him to finish what he was doing, now realising this was the norm around here. Outside I could hear voices, all male. It suddenly dawned on me that I hadn't seen a woman yet. Not that it bothered me, but it did add to the strangeness of the place.

Finally, Captain Wood turned away from his screen and looked at me. 'I believe you came in to see Officer Crane a few weeks ago. We need admin support. Your file was passed on to me.'

I was about to correct him and say it was last week but stopped myself. 'Yes, sir.'

I decided to follow Officer Crane's lead and address the captain as 'sir'.

Wood stood up, revealing an enormous waist, then leaned over to the filing cabinet and brought out a white form. 'When you've finished filling it in, let me know.' He handed it to me and turned back to his computer.

I was a bit taken aback. I thought he would talk a bit about the unit and the roles available to see if I would be interested before handing me a form. Moreover, why did they change their minds and decide to transfer my files to this department? I didn't even know what this department was, other than I was up for an admin post. And why has no one asked to see my CV yet? I thought.

Reluctantly I took the form, which looked fairly straightforward, and filled it out in minutes. Captain Wood swapped it for a sealed brown envelope. 'This is for your medical, follow me.'

Medical?! I got up awkwardly and followed him out, all the time thinking about my hairy legs. He pointed towards the stairs I had just come up. 'Go back through the courtyard, across the other side and you'll see a door down the corridor labelled Medic.'

Why was everything so spread out in this place? I repeated the instructions in my head as I made the journey back down. Now I was really nervous. I had no idea what this medical entailed and why I needed one if I was working in the office. The last time I visited a doctor was twelve years ago and my records were still in Manchester somewhere. I couldn't even remember which surgery or doctor they were with.

The walk to the medic room turned out to be only a few minutes long. I couldn't help noticing how quiet it was. Not a soul in sight. I knocked on the door. No answer.

I knocked again – still no answer. I turned the knob only to be faced with another corridor.

Along I walked, noticing on the left-hand side a door open and the faint sound of a man's voice inside getting louder as I got closer. It was someone talking on the telephone.

'Yeah, mate ... Yeah ... fucking hell. Well, that's the way it goes around here, mate.'

I hovered outside, not sure what else to do, as I needed to check if he was the person I should be speaking to. There wasn't anyone else around.

The conversation continued.

I pressed my back against the wall so he wouldn't see me, as I didn't want to interrupt him but when I heard the receiver click down I quickly knocked on the door.

'Yeah?'

I popped my head around to see a man of medium build with mousy hair. He sat behind a desk with the *Sun* newspaper open in front of him, wearing a canvas jacket and T-shirt. Surely this can't be the medic, I thought.

'I've come for my medical.'

The man looked me up and down a few times. 'Who sent you?' he asked gruffly.

'Captain Wood.'

His eyes moved down to the envelope I was holding, then he put his hand out for it. I stepped into the room and gave it to him. I watched as he ripped it open and scanned through the two sheets of paper inside. I had no idea what was written on them.

Finally he replaced the documents back in the envelope, got up and walked out of the room, brushing my shoulder as he passed.

I stood in the middle of the room and scanned the bare office, clutching my handbag tight. Doubt kicked in, perhaps coming here tonight wasn't a good idea after all. For some reason I had hoped to see the colonel again, but that didn't seem likely.

I checked my watch. I had been here almost an hour and all I'd done was fill out a form.

'Which unit have you come from?'

The man's voice made me jump as he sped back in to the room, still holding my envelope.

'None.'

'Who interviewed you?'

'Captain Wood.'

He turned on his heel. 'This way.'

I followed him out and down the corridor the way

I had come in. His pace was faster than Ginger's, making it impossible to control the clanking noise my heels were making as I tried to keep up.

We entered a room that, thankfully, looked more like a doctor's surgery, with a metal trolley stacked with clear plastic trays and bandages. I looked around, wondering who else was joining.

He closed the door behind and turned to me. 'Let's start by taking off your shoes…'

*   *   *

An hour later, I was heading back up to Captain Wood's office.

The medical wasn't as bad as I thought. I had to accept that things were done differently here and I shouldn't get too hung up, especially at the man's surprise when he saw my hairy legs.

Captain Wood was stood outside his office talking to another man in uniform. They both glanced round at me as I came up the stairs and carried on talking.

I stopped a few metres away and dithered, not knowing what to do with myself except look at the floor. It felt like ages before the man walked off and Captain Wood turned his attention to me.

'OK, Ahmed, come with me.'

I followed him back into the office, watching him go behind his desk, open the same filing cabinet and bring out two green forms.

More forms.

'I need you to fill out these.' He handed them both to me and left the room.

The door was slightly ajar and I could hear faint voices outside. Suddenly a girl appeared; early thirties, tall, broad shouldered, dressed in a dark business suit and with her hair in a bob.

'Is Al in tonight?' she asked with a friendly smile.

'Who?' I asked, looking up from the forms.

'Captain Wood,' she corrected.

'I think he just went out.'

The girl crossed the room to an empty chair close by me.

'I'm Kate,' she introduced, crossing over a muscular leg. 'Haven't seen you before.'

'I just joined.'

'Which unit are you from?'

I shook my head. 'I haven't–'

'Oh…' she cut in. 'You've been doing … other stuff.'

I opened my mouth to reply but she got in before me.

'I'm from Ops Int.,' she continued, shuffling her chair round to face me.

'What's that?'

She looked at me as if I was stupid.

I was saved by a loud knock on the door and another girl appeared. This one was totally different; Amazonian build with blonde hair scraped back and biceps bulging out of her short-sleeved T-shirt. She had the most amazing physique I'd ever seen.

'Hi!' She waved at Kate, not wasting any time. 'I'm Becky. What's your name?' Her accent sounded Australian or Canadian.

Kate looked at her with a cool expression and replied. 'Kate.'

'Hey, Kate! Good to meet you.' Next she pointed at me. 'What's your name?'

'Azi,' I replied quietly, not sure where this conversation was going but pleased to see some females at last.

Becky suddenly dived into a large sports bag that was slung over one shoulder and brought out a family-size chocolate bar.

'Hey, want some?' she asked to no one in particular as she unwrapped half of it.

'No, thanks,' Kate replied, leaning over the desk and taking a copy of *Jane's Defence Weekly*, a military magazine.

Becky pointed the chocolate bar at me, nodding anxiously for me to take a chunk.

I didn't feel like any but felt I should out of politeness, then changed my mind again. I smiled weakly then shook my head, declining her offer.

'Where have you come from?' Kate asked, slowly flicking through pages of the magazine.

Becky swallowed a large piece of chocolate then broke off another before replying, 'I've trained with John and David in Paras, been on climbing expeditions with Martin from here…'

What's Paras?

'Who have you come to see?' Kate scanned down an article.

Becky put another piece of chocolate in her mouth and studied the back of the packet, then reeled out a few more names, none of which included Wood or Crane. Even if she had mentioned them I wouldn't have known – she seemed to know everyone on first-name terms.

I watched the body language between them both. It was as if they had forgotten I was in the room, and by this time I had forgotten about filling out the forms. I had no idea what they were talking about or why they were here, but they definitely didn't look like they were here for admin jobs.

There was another knock on the door and a man appeared holding a clipboard. He looked early forties, a bit taller than me with blond hair and piercing blue eyes, wearing a camouflage uniform.

'Is Al in tonight?' he asked Kate.

'You just missed him.'

The man brushed past Becky and gave her a knowing nod. 'Alright.'

Perhaps this was the Martin she was going on about. Either way, he seemed familiar to both these girls and ignored me.

'Colonel asked me for the list of girls on female selection. Becky, you're down for this … Kate?' he pointed his pen at her.

What's selection? And why is it only for females?

'I want to find out more about it,' Kate replied carefully.

'Come to the meeting next week.'

Then he turned to me.

I looked at him blankly. If these girls were putting their name down, perhaps I should too. I didn't want to give the wrong impression by saying no.

'Yes,' I replied.

Kate and Becky swung round and stared at me, then exchanged glances which made me feel nervous all of a sudden. What had I signed up for?

The man scribbled my name on the clipboard and asked us to report next week with our sports kit. He then strolled out of the room, leaving the three of us in silence.

Moments later Captain Wood was back. I wasn't sure where this left me with the admin post, and when I informed him about the selection training he made no effort to hide his amusement, saying he was sure he'd see me back for my admin post very soon.

CHAPTER FIVE

ALPHA FEMALES

BEFORE THE TRAINING began, I did manage to visit home. I performed the usual routine on the train and changed into shalwar kameez before pulling into Manchester Piccadilly station.

Dad picked me up in his lime-green Mazda. There wasn't much conversation between us but he looked pleased to see me and stroked my head, which was a tradition the elderly did to the young when greeting them. He asked if the journey was OK. I wondered if Mum had mentioned that I had asked after him.

This visit was essential because my sister was back from Pakistan with her shiny new husband and his kid brother. I knew what the brother was here for so I scraped my hair back, wore no make-up and planned to behave as unattractively as possible. That would include giving him dirty looks and improvising pigeon Punjabi to give him the impression that I'd become so Western I could hardly speak my own language any more. My Punjabi was fluent, of course, as I had grown up with it. Thankfully, the marriage bureau hadn't come back with anything yet. I felt a pang of guilt thinking back to my trick with the form filling, but let it go as quick as it came.

I could feel the tension in the house as soon as we arrived. Mum avoided eye contact with me and her words were strained. I wanted the weekend to fly by so I could go back and get on with my new life in the army.

Most of my time was spent serving tea to visitors who, as expected, didn't acknowledge me because they felt I had deserted Mum and Dad. It fuelled Mum to nag me to move back home because I was bringing shame on them. It drove me up the wall along with the Bollywood music blaring out of the TV in the background. I told her to stop talking before I said something I'd regret, but she went on to blame my gobbyness on Dad for not saying anything.

I wanted to ask why she cared what people thought; hadn't she pre-empted this scenario before she said I could go? She herself had shocked both Dad and the community by running her own business, but now that it came to me doing something independent she retreated because of community pressure. I did sympathise, however, because it was she who had to live with the gossip – not me. Although Dad had been through this with the community when she ran the shop and he had dealt with it by ignoring them.

I decided to let it go. I knew Mum was waiting for a reaction to let off steam, and normally she would get one, but I didn't want to get stressed before going back to London. All of this I was managing to keep under control until the weekend ended in a flare up with Shazia. She had finally got in touch and came round to see me. Her dress sense had changed to wearing a full hijab. It was her choice and I respected it.

She was sat a distance away from me and suddenly went into lecture mode about returning home and settling down. I was so angry that she'd turned against me and taken Mum's side.

'What for?' I lashed out. 'To live like you? Anyone can get married and have kids.'

The words came out before I could stop them. I could see the hurt on her face and immediately regretted it. I wanted to apologise but, call it arrogance or pride, I couldn't bring myself to do so. Inside I felt hollow.

I left Manchester feeling ten times worse. Not only

had I left on bad terms with my family, but I had lost my oldest friend. I couldn't remember the last time I'd cried, but that night I poured my heart out on my pillow.

I soon put what was going on in Manchester out of my mind, and when I got back to London, I researched the SAS and what selection training entailed. Luckily, I was sat down. It didn't go into much detail, but what I did find out was enough to make anyone call up and cancel. Though I wanted some physical training, the description I was reading was much more extreme than I'd expected.

The next two days at work were a drag. All I thought about was how I was going to get out of work on time to get to the barracks. I was both excited and scared. Wednesday came around, which was the weekly training evening for selection. I psyched myself up and guiltily left the office early.

Once at the barracks I was directed to one of the classrooms. I was hoping to get an agenda tonight, detailing the course, so that I could remove the fear of the unknown that was killing me inside.

'Come in!' a chorus from inside the room called out when I knocked.

I opened the door to some ten girls sat on plastic chairs in a semicircle. Two familiar faces: Becky and Kate.

For some reason I waved at them and walked over to

an empty chair tagged on the end. No one responded; they all sat in silence staring at a white wall in front of them. My eyes rolled around the room. In the corner there were a pile of cluttered desks, a whiteboard scribbled with notes from a previous class on some weapon descriptions, and a wooden lectern with the 'Who Dares Wins' emblem carved on the front. I remember reading about that quote as the signature of the SAS.

I still wasn't sure what female selection entailed, because none of the research I had done mentioned females.

The door was flung open and in came the clipboard man from last week. He was surprisingly short, now I had a chance to see him again, very lean and slender-framed. He weaved between our chairs and stood at the front.

'Right, ladies.' He flicked through some papers in his hand, making a few of the girls move around in their seats uncomfortably. 'My name is Staff Wright, and I will be taking female selection for any of you who decide to join after tonight. You all know a bit about the selection training we do here with the lads; the colonel wants to do a similar course for girls.'

Firstly I wondered why he was a staff and not an officer or captain – and what staff meant. Secondly, how did the other girls know about the training? Did they do the same research I had or were they 'in the know' by being part of the military? I presumed it was the latter.

'I'll start off by telling you it involves a lot of physical and mental stamina, so if you don't feel up to it you can leave now.'

He paused, enjoying the silence while the girls exchanged glances amongst themselves. I observed in confusion. It was a strange way to introduce a course, but perhaps this was the way things were done to ensure commitment.

I noticed Becky in the front frantically taking notes and wondered if I should be doing the same. I'd brought a fresh notebook with me.

'We have no idea how this will pan out as it's never been done before and we cannot place any benchmark on how far the training will go for you with the lads. So it's going to be as new for us as it will be for you ladies.'

Now it made sense why I couldn't find anything about female selection online or in the material they'd provided, but he still didn't explain why it was taking place, except that the colonel wanted it. Was this the same colonel I'd met during my interview with Officer Crane?

He paused to reorganise his papers, which I thought were handouts for us, but instead carried on talking.

'The information you receive tonight will not leave

this room, and that includes talking to lads in the unit, especially at the bar.'

I didn't understand the last bit about not discussing with people who belonged to the same unit, and didn't realise they had a bar here, but guessed that's where the gossip started.

We listened in silence as he gave us a rundown of the training. It comprised of eight weeks, after which we would join the lads on pre-selection. Pre-selection was the initial training for the lads to test their fitness before being allowed onto the actual selection training course. If we got through pre-selection, we would go onto selection training in the Brecon Beacons.

All this was meant to be part time, but from all the evenings and weekends we were expected to do, I became concerned about how I would fit this in with running the company.

Apparently, out of the 200 or so lads that join up, only a handful get through and go on to the final part of training called continuation, which involves learning how to fight and use weapons, operate on every conceivable terrain and gather intelligence behind enemy lines. Those who got through that would go on to a two-week 'battle camp', after which each survivor would be presented with his SAS beret. This, he explained, was the training for the men.

Staff Wright went on to remind us we were part-timers attempting a challenge designed for the committed – for those who only had one aim in life: to be part of the most elite Special Forces unit in the world. The majority of us wouldn't survive the training, but soon we would have to make a choice between this and our jobs. He also told us to forget what we were outside these barracks, and that we all started from the same place – the very bottom. At twenty-six, I felt old, but here I was the youngest on female selection. To my knowledge, none of the girls was married or had children and each had committed the next year of their life to this training.

'Any questions so far, ladies?' he asked.

Silence.

Why do we have to do an extra eight weeks' training than the lads? I wanted to ask, but felt it was best not to say anything at this early stage.

'Yes?' He pointed his clipboard at someone.

'Would female selection involve classroom work?' a girl asked.

'No is the straight answer. Your training with me is to assess which of you would be physically fit enough to train with the lads.'

'How long will the whole course last?' another piped up.

'As I said before, we have nothing to measure against

but if any of you ladies do get to the end, it would become a thirteen-month course.'

There were a few soft gasps from his audience.

'Ladies,' – Wright put his hands up – 'I'm not going to bullshit you, it's a big commitment physically, mentally, and especially time-wise considering most of you have jobs.' He pointed his clipboard to another girl.

'What will we go on to do if we pass?'

'I can't say any more at this point. The colonel will be coming in during the course and may talk about his plans.'

There were mumbles amongst the girls. I looked around, wanting to join in, but no one was looking my way. He had confirmed what I'd read but hadn't yet given any details of the training sessions.

'OK, ladies,' Wright broke in, 'I want you down in the courtyard in sports kit in fifteen minutes.'

The girls quickly dispersed. I grabbed my bag and followed the girls out because I had no idea where the changing rooms were situated. These girls seemed to know their way around. By the time I got out they were gone.

Panic-stricken, I walked down the corridor past a few blokes who stopped and looked round at me. I asked them if they knew where the girls' changing rooms were, but by the look on their faces I decided not to waste any more time. I quickened my pace, then spotted one girl disappearing down a flight of stairs and went after her.

The changing room was tiny and smelt like it hadn't been used for ages, but, surprisingly, had pink walls. Most of the girls were already changed and stood around in groups chatting about the training. I made a beeline for a quiet spot in the corner and got changed quickly.

I noticed a few girls looking round as I wrapped a towel around my skinny body and tried to get changed underneath it with my bony shoulders sticking out. I felt embarrassed by my body in comparison to their built-up, fuller bodies.

The door suddenly swung open and another girl walked in. 'Is this female selection?' she asked. A couple of girls nodded her way then continued talking.

She came over to where I was and put her sports bag down next to mine. 'I'm Liz,' she said, getting her kit out. I thought she looked like the actress who played Juliet Bravo on TV.

I was surprised by her friendliness, as most of the other girls had not acknowledged me yet, let alone talk to me.

'Which unit are you from?'

'I'm not from another unit.'

She was the fourth person to ask me that question. First it was the officer I registered with, then the medic, then Kate, and now her. 'I'm from Civvy Street,' I replied. I had picked the term up from one of the girls.

Liz put her T-shirt on and winked at me. 'So am I.'

I wanted to believe her but she seemed familiar with the place and had said hello to a few girls on the way in. I looked round and sized them all up. Judging from the posh accents, most were probably officers and fell into two categories: Amazonian and butch. Their legs looked like solid tree trunks, shoulders and biceps like the Incredible Hulk, and they all towered over me. I suddenly panicked; here I stood, 4 ft 11, weighing 7 stone, with no military experience. These girls were scaring the hell out of me, and I hadn't even started training with them yet.

The girls filed out.

Liz tied the shoelaces on her trainers and followed them. 'Come on,' she said. 'We're going to miss all the fun.'

Outside, the courtyard was dark and silent. I was stood in the back rank, copying the others; hands hooked behind my back, legs slightly apart, staring straight ahead. We'd only been out a few minutes and the tips of my fingers pinched from the cold. I wanted to tuck my T-shirt inside my jogging bottoms, but didn't dare move and stand out like the idiot civilian.

Faint voices emerged from the building behind us.

Staff Wright's voice getting clearer on my left, coming round the ranks to the front. He was with another trainer, Staff Taylor, who was, surprisingly, my height, bulky, with a face like a bulldog and a funny left eye. Both were wearing sports kit.

A nervous whisper passed between two girls on my right.

'Listen in,' Taylor growled, his eyes scrutinising each one of us. 'Yes, you in the T-shirt, wanna share the joke? Shut up and listen!'

Silence.

I swallowed a mouthful of saliva, which I'm sure they all heard.

Taylor began walking through the ranks. 'Over the next eight weeks I'll be getting rid of the wasters. Half of you will go tonight.'

My heart was in my throat as he passed by me.

'Your training will not just be confined to these walls; it will be seven days a week. When you're not here you will be running, cycling, swimming, running … and you won't stop until we throw you out. Got it?'

We got it.

I forgot about the cold, then wriggled my toes but couldn't feel them. A part of me wanted to get moving to warm up, but another wanted him to carry on talking to delay the physical training.

Wright glanced at his watch. 'OK, ladies, tonight we'll just do a warm up. Let's go.'

He ran out of the barracks' gates and the girls filed out after him. I was the last one out. The heavens suddenly opened and it poured down. I blinked the rain out of my eyes and ran after everyone onto the King's Road. Wright was at the front setting the pace.

I was second to last running up to Sloane Square station when the girl behind me whizzed past, saying something under her breath about getting a move on. I recognised her from earlier in the changing room, where she had kept staring at me. She had long frizzy hair tied back and looked like her face would crack if she smiled.

My breathing got heavier. I thought I was a good runner; I did OK on a treadmill, but running on hard ground with these girls… I was gasping for air, we'd only been going a few minutes but it felt like ages. The girls were now way ahead, becoming dots in the distance.

The rain was coming down in buckets, making it difficult to dodge the people on the narrow pavement. I weaved between lampposts and parking meters, squinting through my screwed up eyes and trying not to lose sight of them.

Jesus! When do we stop?

Through the black puddles I splashed. My T-shirt was drenched and heavy around the chest, and the beginning of a stitch in my side was excruciating. I wanted to stop but instead pressed a finger down on the side of my waist.

'Widen your strides.' Taylor was suddenly behind me, breathing down my neck loudly.

Out of fear I stretched my legs, taking deep breaths to keep the stitch away. But it wasn't working. The girls ducked into a subway that looked miles away and disappeared. Taylor didn't leave my tail and I knew he wouldn't until I caught up with the rest of them. A few passers-by beneath brollies flitted eyes between me and Taylor, trying to figure it out. I crossed the junction of Brompton Road with Knightsbridge and finally joined the group inside Hyde Park. It was pitch black and deserted. The girls were on the ground doing press-ups.

I tried to calm my breath down and wiped my runny nose with the back of my hand before getting down and joining them. But then they all got up, throwing dirty looks my way. It suddenly dawned on me that Wright had them doing press-ups while waiting for me. I felt terrible putting this burden on them, and worried it would happen each time I was last in.

Wright called us over to where he stood at the edge of a steep bank. 'Two groups, single file.'

I watched the girls quickly form two lines and I followed, shuffling fourth into one of them.

I couldn't think straight or hear what he was saying with all the heavy breathing going on around me, and the rain bashing on my forehead was giving me a headache. I glanced at my watch, hoping the hand had moved on to the next number.

'Go!' Taylor screamed at the first two girls, who jolted into action and sprinted up the bank.

They were powerful, charging up with wide strides. They sprinted around the two trees conveniently located at the top of the hill and ran back down, arms furiously swinging by their sides.

'Go!' Taylor screamed again.

The next two were off before the others got down. I shuffled forward, heart pounding as I watched the first two join the back. Their shocked faces made my stomach churn. I realised how much they had underestimated the short sprint.

'Go!' Taylor's voice rang in my ear.

I sprang forward as fast as I could. My trainers slipped uncontrollably on the muddy bank from the deep footprints left by others. I could feel myself slowing down after the second stride and pressed the palms of my hands down on each thigh to help me up, but the burning sensation in my legs was too much.

'Ahmed!' Taylor shouted from behind. 'What are you doing up there!'

Desperately I tried to catch my breath, closed my eyes and tried not to think of the pain. What were these girls made of? I thought. I pushed my body up, using shorter strides, feeling another stitch coming on as I swung around the tree, where I wanted to collapse in a dizzy spell. Going back down, I suddenly lost control of my feet and fell on my bum. I clutched blades of grass to stop myself slipping as the girls continued running up and dodged around me. I got to the bottom feeling relieved, but also embarrassed, and joined the back of the queue. Within seconds, I was at the front again.

'Go!' Taylor was shouting in my ear.

Two strides up, my legs turned to jelly. I couldn't go on.

'Don't stop!' Taylor shouted after me. 'You've got another eight to go.'

Taylor ended the exercise with a run around the field, leaving me wheezing and wanting to die.

'Right you lot, in pairs. Now!'

I hobbled over to the group and could feel vomit rising up my chest, which I swallowed back down.

'You!' he growled.

My eyes shot open thinking he was talking to me, but it was someone over my shoulder.

'Had enough? Go on, piss off ... waster... The rest of you, on piggy back, now!'

I looked round and watched a girl jog across the field and disappear into the darkness. Before I could figure out which one it was, I felt a crash of weight hit my back. My knees buckled beneath me as I tried to pull the girl's thighs round my hips, but they were so big I could hardly get my hands round them. Somehow she stayed on, but my lower back took all her weight. I squinted at the blurry bench in the distance, which was our target, and dragged one foot in front of the other.

Taylor's voice tannoyed behind, hurling a string of abuse as we raced forward.

Focus. Just focus. Come on.

After a few metres, my legs stopped but my body was still moving forward. The girl on my back thumped my shoulders telling me to hurry up. I recognised the voice from the girl who'd whizzed past me earlier and told me to get a move on – Frizzball. My hands desperately grabbed the flesh of her thighs but it was too late, I fell flat on the ground with my face in the mud, my rib cage crushed by her weight. Frizzball, who I later found out was called Adele, suddenly grabbed a fistful of my T-shirt, pulled me up and swung me over her back. Relieved by the rest, I clamped my arms round her neck, my body jiggling furiously as she ran back to the start point, her pace so powerful I thought I was going to slip off.

We made it back, she let go of my legs, and I dropped in a heap on the ground. I checked my watch; only half an hour had passed. Next, we were ordered into press-up position. I stared down at the blackened grass, inches away from my nose, fingertips dug deep into the cold mud. I had never done press-ups with legs straight before, always with bent knees on a mat in the gym.

'Don't stop.' Taylor's voice was directly above me.

I lugged my body down then back up. One … two – the tips of my trainers were sliding away below – three … four – then my arms began to burn.

I could hear heavy breathing and groaning, not sure if it was me or the girls around – everything blurred into one.

'Shut it! This is not a maternity ward!'

Up … down … up … down…

'And keep your arse down.' Taylor's foot suddenly pushed down over my buttocks.

I froze.

'Faster!' His face slammed down to my level.

My arms jolted into action, sending shooting pains up them. This wasn't training, I thought, it was torture. A part of me wished I'd left when the other girl had.

We were called to our next exercise. I pushed myself up off the ground and staggered over, stopping at the nearest tree to throw up. My eyes watered and it left a sour taste in my mouth. Adele pushed past, sending me flying in the wrong direction. I should get to the front, I thought, picking myself up and following her.

Taylor had been watching me like a hawk all evening and I knew he had it in for me. He'd said he would get rid of half of us tonight and I had to be on his list because I kept coming in last.

We stood in a semicircle, some with our heads between our knees trying to recover from the ordeal, others trying to act normal as their expressions told a different story.

Wright looked at us with a bored expression. 'Listen, ladies, when I tell you to come over, you don't walk. You won't get special treatment when you join the lads.' He pointed across the park at some gates in the distance. 'Leopard crawl to me.'

I watched him run across the field. I couldn't figure out what he meant and looked round at Taylor whose eyes were almost popping out of his head.

'What are you waiting for!?' He screamed at us. 'Move it!'

The girls dropped to their knees, then lay flat on the grass and began to slither like lizards. My heart slumped as I joined them.

'Keep your arse down, Ahmed!'

I dropped my bum as much as possible and dragged

my numb body along the cold, muddy surface. Strands of hair fell over my face out of my ponytail, blinding my vision. I could smell dog poo, and it was strong. I wasn't sure if it was on me but it was following us and making me heave.

Liz passed my left, her muscular arms and legs gliding skilfully across ground.

'They call this a warm up!?' I whispered breathlessly.

She looked round, her face dirty and exhausted. 'You haven't seen anything yet.'

*   *   *

'Walking to the station?' Liz held the changing-room door open for me.

I swung my sports bag over one shoulder and followed her out. I didn't want to walk with her. I needed time on my own. The door slammed close and the noise from the girls inside cut out. My hair was still wet from the cold dribble of a shower, one of my big toes was killing me for some reason and I was walking like a geriatric.

We headed out of the main gates in silence. Usually in these sorts of situations, I would say something to fill the gap but tonight I couldn't. The last two hours had felt like three days. I overheard one girl talking about going back to Hyde Park tomorrow to do the same circuit. This place was full of nutters.

'Good night, ladies.' The security guide smiled at us both as we passed his Portakabin. I recognised him from earlier. He was the only person who smiled around here.

I wondered about next week and how I would get through another torturous session. Who could I talk to about it? We were ordered not to talk to anyone about this training, but I guessed a few of the girls had told their boyfriends or family. My friends wouldn't believe me, let alone understand if I told them I'd joined the army and signed up for this training. As for my family, there was enough going on there without this to complicate matters even further.

'Fancy a drink?'

Liz's offer took me by surprise. I began thinking up an excuse but it was too late, she was already crossing the road.

I followed behind, dodging the traffic. 'Are there any coffee shops round here?'

'Coffee?' Liz rolled her eyes. 'You're really pushing the boat out.'

We headed into Blushes Café opposite the barracks and grabbed a table at the front. I checked my phone; no missed calls from home or from Shazia. I didn't want to call any of them to apologise. I hadn't done anything wrong.

The waitress placed a cup of coffee down in front of me and a large glass of red wine for Liz. I gulped the warm liquid, staring across at Liz slowly sipping her wine and looking out of the window, watching the other girls leave the barracks and head up to Sloane Square. I thought about telling her what I'd heard Adele say earlier in the changing rooms when I was coming out of the showers: 'That Asian is a slacker', said loud enough for me to hear. But I didn't want to come across as weak and moany in front of Liz, so decided not to say anything.

'When will they let us know if we got through?' I asked.

'You did,' she assured me, 'and whoever else decides to turn up next week. Female selection is voluntary withdrawal, which is harder than being kicked out.'

I thought about it for a moment and realised she was right. I remember an incident when I was about ten when Dad challenged me to carry a sack of rice upstairs for fifty pence. After the second stair, my body couldn't take it but I kept going for an hour. Not for the money but because I didn't want to be seen as a failure by anyone, most of all myself.

The waitress came over with another glass of red and swapped it for Liz's empty one. 'What do your parents think of you joining the army?' Liz asked, holding my gaze.

I looked away, wishing I'd gone home now. I knew this would come up because my surname was Muslim. What was I meant to say? They don't know and I never intend telling them? I didn't want to get into a full-blown debate about religion, women and culture. I was sick of having to justify what I did in life because of the family I was born into. Why couldn't people take me at face value? Why did everyone seem to think there was some big drama attached to anything different that I did? I didn't want to be a special case with the army and give them an excuse to tell me I was useless.

'They're fine about it,' I lied. 'I just didn't say which unit I was in.'

Liz went on to ask a ton of questions; where my family lived, what my parents do, whether any of my siblings were in the army.

She was sizing me up, I concluded. I wasn't a ranking officer, had no military experience and didn't speak with a posh accent. The only thing I could do was to glamorise my dad's time in the British Indian Army by describing him as an officer, although I had no idea if this was true. I quickly changed the subject by asking if she was joining the others at Hyde Park.

'I've got to work,' she replied looking around the room. 'But you should go.'

She was right, I had to get fitter – much fitter – but I

wasn't going to gatecrash the girls' club. I had to devise my own training regime.

The evening ended with Liz giving me a rundown of the unit and what she knew about female selection. The colonel heading the training turned out to be the man I'd met at my interview. I suddenly realised how lucky I was to be a part of all this. Everything I'd achieved over the years wouldn't come close to this if I got through. It was the chance of a lifetime and I had already decided I would be going back next week.

The next day I crawled out of bed, my stomach muscles hurting as I breathed in and out. I checked for bruising but there were no signs of last night's ordeal. It all felt like a surreal dream now, including Liz. I started to think about how I was going to train – I could hardly move my body let alone do a three-hour circuit tonight, and there was no chance of wearing heels to work today.

The week didn't get any better, especially as Wednesday crept up on me. I got mood swings, couldn't sleep at night and lay awake thinking about how much fitter the other girls would be than me and how I would cope with another beasting.

On Wednesday, I was up early and prayed to Allah to get me through the training that night. In the office, I spent the morning staring at the computer screen, couldn't eat my lunch then mentally argued with myself not to go in. The afternoon dragged torturously and by then I just wanted to get the evening over with.

Five thirty finally struck and I was out of the door. I lied to people in the office that I had a doctor's appointment. Usually I wouldn't leave the office before eight. On the way to the barracks, I grabbed some fries from McDonald's and sat at a table of noisy kids, forcing them down. My stomach was acidic from the two cups of coffee I'd had that day.

Twenty minutes later, I was back in the dark courtyard wearing sports kit. Liz was standing in the front rank. I couldn't thank her enough for saving my life tonight. With all the faffing around this morning, I had forgotten to pack my jogging bottoms. Luckily, she had a spare pair of shorts.

Staff Wright was stood at the front, counting us with his eyes. 'We're five short, any more to come?'

The response was silence, so he led us out once more.

My eyes skimmed the blackened skyline as we entered Hyde Park. A memory floated to the surface of my mind – my first summer in London as a student; strolling across the green, passing an array of romantic couples, Arab families and teams of people playing rounders and football. My head was tilted towards the warm sun. I had smiled to myself, thinking what a different world this was to the kebab shop.

Staff Wright's screaming broke into my dreamy consciousness. Three torturous hours later, after the same circuit as last time, we were back in the barracks courtyard. We got down to press-up position. My fingers had turned white. I couldn't feel my body and my stomach felt like a big hole had been cut out of it.

Ten press-ups turned to twenty, then forty, then eighty…

I closed my eyes and tried to block the pain, but it kept coming back. My senses became blurry and a strange humming sound went off in my head. Just as I thought I was about to pass out, we were dismissed. I dashed to the changing rooms, grabbed my bag and headed out, still wearing my soggy sports kit. I needed to be on my own for the training ordeal to sink in. Liz said something to me as I passed her but I ignored it. A part of me wanted to make an excuse not to come in next week, but the reality was that I didn't have a choice. I would be failing myself, which was harder to live with than getting through this training.

The week flew by and I was back at the barracks. Most of my paperwork for becoming a member of the Territorial Army had gone through and I was given an army number. My security clearance was taking longer to come through than the others'; I didn't question it but it did play on my mind. The army number was like a new identity, a sense of belonging to an establishment, which I didn't feel when I received my national insurance number. I'm a squaddie, I thought proudly. No I'm not, I corrected myself, I don't burp or fart in the company of others, nor do I have a partner with peroxide hair, which most of the male squaddies have. I'm a private – Private Ahmed.

Getting the number somehow changed my mental state. I got tougher with my training regime. I walked into work every day carrying a rucksack weighed down with books to strengthen my legs. I trained every day in the gym except the evening before barracks, when I gave my body a rest. Liz started taking me to kickboxing and got me punching so hard I could hardly uncurl my fingers afterwards. She said I wasn't aggressive enough and tried to teach me to switch off my emotions, which became a challenging exercise.

Over the weeks, I felt my body change; it became stronger but I wasn't putting on any weight. In fact, I was losing it, now weighing 6.5 stone. My appetite increased, though I still had difficulty eating breakfast, which had been a problem since childhood.

I began to leave the office early on a regular basis and received the silent treatment from colleagues, but I didn't care. They would never understand what the army meant to me, how it enriched my life more than this job. I began to view life differently. No longer did I feel the need to please the people at work.

Over the weeks, the number of girls dwindled down and the training became more intense, with less chatter in the changing rooms. Then something terrible happened, Liz didn't turn up one week. I sent her a couple of text messages to meet up but all I got back was radio silence. I was gutted. Training wasn't the same without her but I had to keep going, female selection was almost complete.

I got to know the other girls from a distance. Adele turned out to be not only scary but loud as well. She reminded me of my mum's friend Auntie Pataani but without the rolls of fat and laughter. I learnt to accept her blanking me. The only time she would say something was when she had an audience to criticise me in front of. Sometimes when we stood in a long line, on parade awaiting training instructions, she would look round at me to check I was in position properly then roll her eyes at the other girls.

Then there was Specky, who had been in the army for quite some time, chewed gum and wore glasses that made her eyes looked massive. She talked openly about her previous training and 'survival tactics' that involved killing animals, cutting them up and eating them, which made me feel sick. She was good friends with another recruit who looked the most experienced and oldest of the group. I called her Blondie because I never really got to speak to her or find out her name. She was in her late thirties and was very quiet.

Andrea was the 'it' girl who worked in the military as a medic. All the girls were nice to her because she was engaged to a man in the regular SAS.

I came to realise that most of the girls were of officer status. Some, like Liz and Kate, didn't make a big deal about their achievements, but others wanted to shout about it and remind the privates what rank they were. Caroline was tall, intelligent and stuck up and wore a Cambridge University sweatshirt that had seen better days. She hung close to another officer who had a lot of clout – I had no idea what her name was but she never smiled so I named her Ice Maiden.

Then there was Jenny, who drank pints of Guinness and drove the big four-ton army trucks. She didn't seem to take the training seriously: I only saw her there for two weeks then she didn't turn up again.

Finally, if there was one girl we all knew would get through, it was Becky, the South African international champion rock climber. She was the fittest of us all and every girl knew it.

Every now and then, my mind would wander back to Mum and how I had left it with her the last time I was home. It wasn't her fault, she didn't know what was going on in my life and was only trying to do what was right. I swallowed my pride and called her. I was relieved to hear her voice, though the demand to return was still there. I stayed calm by switching off. I only cared about getting through female selection, a feeling no one would understand. I was waking up in the morning thinking about it and closing my eyes at night dreaming of it. It was emotionally torturous, the effect was like a drug, but it was now my world.

CHAPTER SIX

THE OTHER WORLD

T HE TRAIN PULLED into Manchester Piccadilly station and I was up before everyone, clutching my small bag and making a beeline for the doors. I hated this part of the journey; the walk to the bus stop, waiting ages for the bus, then the hour-long journey back to my parents' house.

Nothing changed around here and my mind switched modes accordingly. I was back home, things slowed down, life became simpler and I needed to behave more subserviently.

I looked out of the window as the bus drove past the familiar shops and roads. There was a pub on every block, something I hadn't noticed when living here.

What surprised me about the army was how the drinking culture was engrained into their daily lives. It was both a means of bonding and an outlet for socialising. It took me a while to get my head around it but realised it was similar to the social gatherings we had growing up, of which chai, rather than beer, was the main component.

A few women with screaming kids got on the bus looking bad tempered, their clothes and hair worn carelessly. This was a daily occurrence when I lived here but today it felt like a distraction. I watched them throwing the prams into the luggage carrier, talking loudly as they took their seats, and then I suddenly recognised one of them from school. I felt embarrassed for thinking she was a woman, as I still saw myself as a girl. More surprisingly, I remembered her being one of the clever ones in our year. She would sit at the back of class messing around but then flew through her exams without much effort. She could have become anything she wanted. I wanted to go over and say hello but wasn't sure where the conversation would go. Would she be happy to see me or still too annoyed with her kids to spark off a conversation? I knew for sure she would be shocked if I told her I lived in London and still wasn't married. It was a given that Pakistani girls got married off as soon as they left school. Maybe she wouldn't recognise me out of my school uniform, I convinced myself, and decided to stay put.

I was wearing a pale blue shalwar kameez under my Puffa jacket. It was free flowing and comfortable. My training shoes beneath looked unfeminine but my feet were too sore for girly ones. Nowadays all my clothes hung off me and I worried that Mum would notice the weight that had dropped off my face. I'd caught her looking at me strangely a few times in the past few months. If anything, I should be putting *on* weight coming into my late twenties, but I seemed to be going the other way.

Perhaps it was the stress; there was a lot going on and my head was buzzing. I thought about my training, the business and my future. Part of me wanted to walk away from the company because work colleagues had noticed my attention span dwindling in the office, which was not good for morale. However, at the same time, the sentimental side of having set it up from my bedroom and then watching it grow had made me cling on.

I wasn't concerned about being financially stable any more. I was drawing a minimum wage from the business and cash flow was tight but it didn't matter as long as I had enough to keep me afloat during training. I thought back to that first meeting at the barracks and the officer's comment about having to make a choice sooner or later. In the past, I had balanced much more in my life, but this was something out of the ordinary and most definitely didn't feel part time. Was it worth the risk of leaving the company now? What were the chances of getting through to the next phase of training? Adding a further complexity, I was still waiting for my security clearance to come through. I made regular visits to the admin department to check, but each time got the silent headshake from Captain Wood. It was strange going back up there and seeing him. Perhaps something unexpected had come up about my family background that was causing the delay. I didn't know much about my relatives in Pakistan as I hadn't been over since I was a baby and I couldn't exactly ask my parents if there was anyone dodgy.

I imagined Becky and the others out doing a ten-mile run and felt lazy sat on a bus. I would never be as fit as they were, but I needed to keep my fitness up to a level that meant I could survive without getting injured.

I wished that I could talk to someone about all these dilemmas. I thought about Shazia. She had always been the one I could reach out to no matter how contrasting our lives were and she was also very discreet, which was unique in our community. There was a time when she didn't pass judgement, but now she nagged me as if she was my mother.

I wished I could tell Dad but I knew that was impossible. Even if I did tell him, he wouldn't believe me; nobody around here would – they'd think I was a nutter. Besides, it wasn't worth risking, especially now my parents were off to Mecca. It would be the biggest journey they would take together, apart from their marriage; a completion of their lives before going to heaven and I was still racking my brains for an excuse not to go with them – they were still under the impression that I would be joining them.

I jumped off the bus, in a world of my own, and suddenly was stopped by Scott, an old customer who was getting on.

'Hiya,' he said, folding up a buggy as his girlfriend got on with a baby.

It was nice to see familiar faces. I wasn't sure if they looked older or just tired but they weren't the fresh-faced couple I used to see going to the pub. I wondered how I looked to them and then caught my reflection in the side mirror of the bus. I had no make-up on and my skin looked dry. I looked down at my hands: my nails were broken, and underneath each was a line of deeply embedded dirt that would not come out no matter how much I scrubbed. Quite a contrast to my floral years at college, when I would match my jewellery, butterfly eyeshadow and nail varnish.

I arrived home and to my dismay could hear Auntie Pataani talking to Mum in the living room. I recognised her loud, screechy laughter as soon as I came in through the front door. I didn't want to go inside so instead pressed my ear to the living-room door. I could hear her gossiping about someone's daughter who'd run off with an English boy. This woman never ceased to amaze. There she was, tarnishing families in their difficult times when her own daughter had married someone she'd met at college and had stopped speaking to her.

I heard Mum trying to interject a few times about the plans for hajj, then it suddenly came to me. Auntie Pataani had been widowed for ages and had always wanted to go on hajj. As a woman, though, she was not allowed to go without the presence of a husband, father, brother or son. If none of these were available, only then could a close male friend, acting as a brother, accompany her. She was a complete pain in the arse but perhaps I could persuade my parents to take her instead of me. This would guarantee them all a place in heaven. Pleased with my brainwave, I entered the living room with confidence.

Auntie Pataani was sprawled over the settee, head propped up on one of Mum's plump cushions, eating her way through a bowl of rice pudding. She waved me over, making a big deal about how terrible I looked since leaving home, asking how long I was home for, how I should be looking after my parents now they were getting old, and how she'd heard that I'd be going on hajj with them. It all came out in one breath. I reckon she was long overdue to go home but had waited for me to get here just so that she could stir things up with me and Mum. I'd never forget her efforts to change Mum's mind about me studying in London. She'd even got as far as bringing a woman over whose son had studied away and had ended up marrying a Chinese woman who, according to her, ate snakes and cats.

I wanted to retaliate by asking Auntie Pataani if *her* daughter was at home looking after her, let alone her son who had long gone. But I would never cross the line with my parents' friends no matter what they said.

I stood in the middle of the room between them both and turned to Mum. I opened my mouth to talk about the hajj trip but was prevented from doing so by Auntie Pataani twittering on about something behind me. I turned round, trying to stay focused on what she was saying … something about making sure I looked after my parents when they came down to London next week.

I nearly had a heart attack. Mum intervened, reiterating what Auntie Pataani had said, confirming that she and Dad were planning to come and visit some friends in Croydon.

Before I could say anything, Auntie Pataani tugged the hem of my dress and pulled me back. She was now sitting up on her big bum and telling me it was her idea that my parents stay with me, for respect, otherwise people here would gossip that they couldn't stay with their daughter. I wanted to kill her. The only tongue that would wag was hers, I was sure! She didn't deserve to go to heaven, I suddenly decided.

I should have stopped there and waited until she'd gone home to discuss it further with Mum, but the panic had already set in. I told Mum I had to work and perhaps it was best if they went directly to Croydon and stayed there. Mum mulled over it for a moment, pressing a maroon fingernail into the dimple of her cheek, and then agreed. I was relieved. Then stupid Auntie Pataani poked her nose in and suggested that, since the visit to Croydon would be during the day, they could see me in the evening after 'work'. Mum changed her mind and agreed with Auntie Pataani.

I didn't know what to say; they both had me in a corner. But I couldn't miss the training, not now. Suddenly the hajj story didn't seem as urgent any more. I needed to thrash out some convincing excuse for them not to come and see me – fast. The thought of their first visit to London had haunted me since the start of female selection. They'd never asked before. I needed to go and see Shazia.

'Who is this Shazia?' Auntie Pataani asked, surprised she'd never heard of her before.

'You know,' Mum said, 'the one who runs the Urdu classes for children at mosque.'

'Ah yes.' Auntie Pataani looked relaxed again. 'The good girl ... your other daughter's friend.'

I decided not to waste my time. I was now beginning to think this woman had no idea how tactless she was.

The evening ended with a visit from yet another family, which meant I couldn't see Shazia until the morning.

Dad had made his excuses about some late delivery at the shop, which left Mum to run the show. I got changed into some glitzy outfit Mum had put out for me to wear and entered the living room.

'My daughter's a manager,' Mum cooed, and sank into the armchair, patting the empty chair beside her.

I crossed the room and did as I was told, trying to avoid eye contact with the man sat on the large sofa close to his mother. Too close.

He watched me with hard brown eyes. Mid-thirties, I guessed, judging by his clean-shaven coffee complexion and perfectly drawn side parting in his hair.

The smell of rose-scented cream drifted across from the gentle-looking woman wearing a pale yellow headscarf over long grey hair and matching cotton suit. She smiled kindly as she prepared a cup of tea and handed it to her son.

I smiled back then looked over to the other sofa, which was lined with four sisters, all wearing brightly coloured silk suits with costume jewellery and gold woolly socks. They cased me up and down.

'My daughter works for a very big company. Just like your son, Nasser.' Mum reached for the plate of shortbread biscuits on the table and handed it to one of the girls. The girl took one and passed the plate down.

'What do you do?' Nasser asked with a northern twang.

I looked at Mum blankly, then back at him. 'I work for an internet company,' I replied.

The room went quiet. All I could hear was the crunching of biscuits coming from the girls' corner.

Nasser nodded approvingly, taking a sip of tea, and then handed the cup and saucer back to his mother.

I watched his mother make the exchange and offer a plate of Indian sweets to him, which he waved a dismissive hand to, his eyes still on me.

'A manager,' he repeated. 'Where did you do your degree?'

Was this some kind of interview?

'London,' I replied flatly, dropping the polite expression for a hard stare back.

He nodded again, leaning back and resting an ankle on his knee, revealing stripy brown socks and black shiny shoes. 'Does it pay well?'

Who was this man?

I didn't reply.

'Does it pay well?' he repeated.

I didn't answer his question but instead smiled sweetly and asked, 'What do you do?'

The room fell quiet. The girls' jaws dropped, his mother looked fearful for her son, and Mum burst into nervous giggles.

'I'm a banker,' he said, and cleared his throat.

More like a wanker, I thought. 'Which bank?'

'High street.'

My mouth curled up at the ends. Not quite an investment banker then...

He shuffled around in his seat and looked at his mother.

'Times have changed, sister.' Mum gave me one of those glares I got as a kid that meant I should shut up.

'My son is very Western,' Nasser's mother said glowingly, trying to rescue the conversation. 'He will only marry a girl who has a university degree and a good job. His father would be very proud if he was alive today.'

'God willing,' Mum dramatically raised her hands up to the ceiling in prayer position, 'both our children will be married soon.'

I looked at Nasser's mother. He doesn't want a wife, I thought, he just wants a replacement for you.

The next morning I headed to Shazia's. The walk from the bus stop was agonising on my feet. I had spent ages in the bathroom covering them with Vaseline and plasters before coming out. I'd been recommended all sorts of ointments to soothe bruising and blisters at the barracks, but Vaseline was the only thing I relied on.

I didn't bother ringing her before coming over and hoped she would be in. After I'd knocked on the painted blue door of her house, I looked down the street while I waited for her to answer. This place hadn't changed in the years I'd been gone. I still recognised the same plastic flowers in some of the windows, including those in Shazia's old house, which I'd just walked past. I wanted to go in and say hello to her mum but felt it best to make peace with Shazia first, just in case I heard something I didn't like and arrived at Shazia's in the wrong mood. I couldn't be doing with another nagging.

I heard some noisy kids come out of the mosque across the street. I saw a five-year-old girl hurriedly putting her shoes on and running to her mum, who was stood outside with the rest of the mothers.

Childhood memories flooded back of my mum coming to pick me up when I was that age. The hostile welcome she got from the Bangladeshi women, all huddled together in a sea of colourful saris. Mum didn't care; she'd walk straight up to them in her Pakistani shalwar kameez and start talking.

A man then came out of the mosque after the kids and, to my surprise, it was my old imam from all those years ago. He looked different; his beard was now parted in two and curled up at the ends; was coloured with henna to make it orange. He looked vulnerable; his back was hunched forward and he moved slowly with the aid of a stick, using the other frail hand to thumb through a tasbih. His eyes still watered and his clothes still hadn't seen an iron. I wondered if his caning skills were still as good.

I had not read Arabic since leaving mosque and wondered how quickly it would come back if I decided to attempt it now, though my pronunciation would still be like that of a child. It suddenly occurred to me how Christians finish their prayers with 'Amen' and at mosque we finish our prayers with '*Ameen*'. Was this the same? Also, the headscarves worn in mosque were the same as the ones worn by Christian women during Lent.

What would life be like if I hadn't had that confrontation with Mum about wanting to study away? Perhaps I'd be one of these women picking up my kids. What if I hadn't made that spontaneous visit to London? Bristol would not have given me the Chelsea Barracks…

My thoughts were interrupted by the sound of the

latch sliding off the hook from inside the door, and then Shazia's face appeared. She was wearing a scarf wrapped tightly around her head and was holding a wooden spoon. Her face dropped for a split second when she saw me.

'Hiya,' I said as I stepped inside and embraced her stiff shoulders, grabbing her loosely fitted purple dress. I could smell cooking turmeric coming from the back of the house.

'How are you?' she asked, trying to pull away.

I caught the undercurrent in her voice. 'Good, thanks. I thought I'd come and see you.'

She led me down the long narrow hallway lit by a single bulb at the top of the stairs. It was dark and cold but then got brighter and warm as we entered the kitchen. A couple of pans bubbled away on the stove, steaming up a window above. The sink looked chaotic, covered in half-cut vegetables and packets of spices scrunched up. I couldn't stand untidiness growing up, and the army had taught me to be minimal and compact.

The soles of my shoes stuck to the lino as I walked over to the small wobbly table and sat down. I watched her putting a pan of water on to make chai. She threw sugar, full-fat milk and spices into it then served it up to me in a Smarties mug. I didn't like chai, even when I lived at home. She knew that.

After the initial awkwardness, to my relief, the

conversation finally began to flow between us like we were old friends again. She told me about how her husband's business was 'booming' and about the new car they were planning to buy (which I wasn't interested in at all but nodded every so often anyway). All the time I was thinking of how to approach the subject of the army, hajj, my delayed security clearance, my parents' visit to London and my sanity.

'Your mother's been through enough as it is,' Shazia cooed. 'You're not helping matters by being so … picky.'

I looked the other way, feeling helpless.

'Kashif sounds like a nice boy.' Shazia tried to look serious. 'When are you next seeing him?'

You probably know more than I do, I wanted to say, but resisted. Kashif was another potential suitor my mother had lined up. Admittedly he looked like golden boy compared to that idiot from last night.

I decided to stop wasting time.

'Shazia,' I cut in. 'I need to talk to you.'

She smiled at me, her eyes softened. 'I was waiting for you to ask. I've noticed you're not looking yourself these days.'

I studied her carefully. For a split second I got worried. Was she going to tell me something I didn't want to hear? I brushed the negative thoughts to one side and decided to trust in her.

'Thank you,' I whispered, reaching out and touching the silk sleeve of her dress. I felt terrible for all those resentful thoughts I'd had about her. I should have picked up the phone and shared the burden as soon as it became too much to bear alone.

'I was also nervous on my wedding night.' She broke into a cheesy grin. 'Men are like bears…'

It shouldn't have surprised me. I decided to change tactics and talk about London and my company. She looked pleased for me so I carried on and mentioned my spare time and taking up a hobby.

'Another college course?' she assisted.

I laughed nervously, half expecting her to come out with something so obvious. I shook my head and started jabbering on about something more 'physical'.

She looked round, bemused, then pointed a finger at me and started to laugh aloud. 'Don't you think you're a bit old for that?'

The resentment came back. I felt hurt by her belittling comment. No, I wanted to shout back, I don't feel old, no matter what stage in life people expected me to fit into. I realised her attack on me last time wasn't a one-off. This was who she'd become since being married. She thought she knew better than I did. She didn't care what I did any more, but then again, I didn't care about her life either, I realised guiltily.

'Mum and Dad want me to go to hajj with them.'

'Yes, I heard … me and my husband are hoping to go when the business picks up,' she prattled.

She had told me the business was booming before, but I let it go. It wasn't the first time she had exaggerated and most definitely wouldn't be the last.

'I can't go,' I blurted. 'I don't have time with the business.'

'Of course you can, my father-in-law got my husband to look after the shop when he went.'

'It's not a shop.'

'Think of all the respect you'll get around here if you go. All the bad things people have been saying about you will be forgotten.'

Most of them coming from you, I was tempted to add, but kept my mouth shut. 'I don't care what people think.'

'Your parents do.'

There was an uncomfortable silence. I could see this going into lecture mode like last time and decided to retreat from the whole discussion. It had been a wasted journey coming here today.

I stood up to leave, then stopped as I tuned to the noise coming from the neighbouring wall. It was chanting mixed with wailing.

'What's that?' I pointed to the house next door.

'Shi'ites,' Shazia said as she wrinkled her nose,

reminding me of Julie from school when I had the spicy omelette sandwich. 'They're doing the Ashura; punishing themselves for the mistake they made of believing that the Prophet's son-in-law, Ali, should have taken over after Mohammed's death – instead it was Abu Bakr, Mohammed's father-in-law, who did.'

I didn't want to get into a debate, but ever since I'd been on my religious journey, discovering other faiths and facing difficult truths, I had to say something.

'I don't think it is a punishment,' I replied.

Shazia grabbed a big knife and started chopping up a bunch of coriander. 'Just because you've been to uni doesn't make you above us lot.'

'You lot?' I forced a laugh. 'Just because you live here doesn't mean you know it all.' I gulped the chai. It tasted disgusting.

'You have no idea what it's been like for us.'

I wasn't sure if she was talking about being Sunni, a woman or Pakistani and frankly didn't care. I hadn't come here to listen to this, but couldn't stop myself. 'You think that by living in London my life is easier?' I snapped back. 'I still get it all the time on the phone from Mum, thanks to you.'

There, I'd said it. It felt like a weight off my shoulders. But, at the same time, I wish I'd kept my mouth shut. I could tell from her face there was no forgiveness for me this time. But did I care? I tried to find compassion inside me, and then it finally came. Her life was these four walls and cooking for the men of the house, who were hardly ever home. She had no children to keep her company, and that would be putting tremendous strain on her marriage, not to mention the tongues that would be wagging in the community. She was expected to have become pregnant in the first year of marriage, with a son. I was away from it all and only got snippets when I visited, which stressed me out, but imagine having this 24/7, I thought. This wasn't my mess, however, and I didn't want to be burdened with it; I had enough going on and needed someone to listen to me.

I left Manchester feeling ten times worse, with no idea how to stop my parents coming to London, and no idea who to talk to. The train journey back was a nightmare. Three hours turned to six because of track delays, or so they said. I was still wearing the glitzy outfit under my Puffa jacket and couldn't be bothered to go to the toilet and get changed into jeans. I was knackered. The house had been like Piccadilly Circus last night with guests coming and going, visiting Mum and Dad to talk about their spiritual journey. The last one left around midnight, then Mum and I cleared up. I got up early this morning to clean the house before leaving. Thankfully, I didn't see any more of Auntie

Pataani that weekend. She was like an irritating rash I'd had all my life. I wasn't sure who was worse, her or Taylor.

My legs felt stiff from sitting down too long so I got up and hobbled over to the catering carriage on the train. There was a queue at the snack bar and they were giving out complimentary teas and coffees as recompense for the delay we were experiencing. I didn't want either – I wanted to eat again. I joined the queue and stared out of the window at the rolling hills and meadows. The sun was shining down on me but I felt grim.

I tried to morph my mind back to the barracks but it kept flipping to the events of the weekend at home. My anxiety to go out for a 10-mile run had long gone. I didn't think Shazia would ever speak to me again, or should I say I would never speak to her. It wasn't my fault her life had ended up like it had. If she'd been braver, stood up to her mum and taken the risk like I had, her life may have mapped out differently.

My eyes prickled with sadness. I was going to miss Dad when he went to hajj. I did manage to get some time with him before leaving and asked if he was looking forward to going. He nodded, but interestingly he didn't ask if I was. Perhaps he could read me better than Mum or maybe it was just that, unlike her, he wasn't in denial. I just wish he'd voice himself more. If only

I could tell him about my army life, then all my problems would be resolved; he would manage Mum and fight off all the obstacles going forward.

They planned to be back in six weeks, by which time I would either be off the training or on the hills, which would mean another difficult conversation with them. I wondered if the other recruits' lives were as complex. At least they could tell their families they were in the army, which was half the battle for me. But perhaps the lads had other pressing issues that I didn't encounter, like kids. I couldn't imagine the strain the training might put on a relationship.

A bloke brushed past me. He stood by the window and checked his phone. He was wearing jeans and trainers with a very large outdoorsy rucksack hanging off one shoulder. I did a double take, suddenly recognising him from the barracks. He was often hanging outside Captain Wood's office when I'd go up to check on my security clearance papers and would look at me like he'd taken a bad turn in a bad neighbourhood.

I should have gone back to my carriage and everything would have been fine, but instead I moved along with the queue to the front of the bar. My heart was pounding. I tried to look in every direction except at him. The lady behind the counter was very loud and chirpy which didn't help. She was also taking her time serving, making me stand across from the lad for what felt like ages while queuing.

Then the inevitable happened. The lad got distracted and looked up straight at me. Neither of us moved, then his eyes lowered to check out my outfit and back up to my sparkly shawl wrapped around my neck, half covering my head. I wasn't sure who was more surprised, me or him. For some reason I didn't want him to see me dressed like this. Perhaps if I'd been wearing jeans I would have tried to initiate a conversation. My mind went back to secondary school when I'd see classmates in town on Saturday. I'd be out of uniform, wearing traditional clothes while shopping with Mum. I'd wave at them but they would blank me as if embarrassed to be associated with me.

A heavy stillness hung between me and the lad. Everything stopped around us, as he witnessed a snippet of my other world. I wasn't sure if I should say hello or lead him to believe it was mistaken identity, but either way it left us both in a very strange place.

CHAPTER SEVEN

JOINING THE LADS

'WHERE'S THE THIRD?' Staff Monty flicked his eyes between me and Becky. He was talking about Adele, who was meant to be joining us. It was a Friday night and we were stood in the courtyard of the Chelsea Barracks in what was becoming the usual weather; dark, wet and a fierce, cold wind.

Monty was our new trainer on pre-selection. He was a tall, lanky man who looked like the lead singer from Spandau Ballet. His seriousness wasn't as convincing as the other trainers because of his soft features, but his voice boomed.

He had trained us a few times at Hyde Park, running

alongside me and ordering me to widen my strides. I definitely felt my fitness level escalate during this time, and knew that the gap between me and the other recruits was getting smaller.

I'd bought myself a Helly Hansen top. I'd never been to an outdoor shop before but we'd been advised to buy one. They also asked us to buy a training bag but I couldn't afford it so used my wash bag instead, which was awkward to run around with. We'd been issued with our uniform. It was huge on me so I had to go down to see George who managed the stores, where all the army supplies were kept, to get it taken in, as well as pick up my size four boots that had to be specially ordered. George had a warm, round, gentle face, and he reminded me of a teddy bear.

I hadn't been sleeping well ever since getting back from Manchester and during the day I carried a nauseous feeling around in my stomach. Since getting back to London I had attempted to call home a few times with excuses to avoid my parents on their visit to London, but couldn't think of any. In the end I had cowardly left a message on their answering machine the day they planned to visit, telling them that I would be away on a training course all weekend. I should have spoken to them, but didn't have the bottle. It left me with the fearful thought that they would arrive at my empty flat in a few hours' time while I was still here. I'd also been having bad dreams, which I don't normally remember, but this one was reccurring: running through a forest surrounded by a pack of wolves, my hair all over the place blinding my vision. I would try to keep up but then would trip over and be pulled back up by the wolves that dragged me along like a rag doll.

'As from tonight, you'll be joining the men.' Monty pointed his finger at me and Becky. 'It's going to be a tough weekend. I don't want you anywhere near them except during training. They need to stay focused.'

I couldn't believe what I was hearing. What did he think *we* were going to do to hinder *them*?

We were dismissed. I picked up my wash bag and followed Monty and Becky towards the glowing headlights of the white minibus parked just inside the gates. I felt scared, not sure what to expect. Maybe Adele was already in there. I had a feeling she was going to make my life hell. She and Becky were going to become a 'pair' and I would be left on my tod. Maybe she saw me as an embarrassment and expected a better calibre to be training alongside her.

The sinking feeling stayed with me as I clambered into the van where the lads were sat in khaki T-shirts. There was a horrible tension. I didn't know what was worse, being here or calling Mum when I got back.

The lads looked up as we got in and then turned away. Monty had probably had a word with them, I thought, settling down next to a lad whose forehead was pressed against the window. He had red blotches on the nape of his shaven head and reminded me of the lads who used to hang outside my school.

The vehicle roared out of the barracks. I looked down at my wash bag and started playing with its metal clip, worrying that I wasn't as physically fit as Becky and Adele. Earlier, in the changing rooms, I couldn't help but stare at Becky's strong physique as she stood in front of the sink, combing back her hair. I would have liked to cut my hair short so it would be easier to manage during training but instead had to spend ages putting it into tight braids. Long hair was a sign of femininity in our culture and Mum would kill me if I cut it. I stared out into the darkness. It was just forty-eight hours, I told myself, but in army terms that felt like a lifetime.

I tried to sleep for part of the journey but didn't succeed, and neither did any of the others. We arrived at Pirbright Barracks just after midnight. As soon as the vehicle parked up, all hell broke loose.

Everyone shot up to get out as fast as they could. I let a few pass me then asked myself why I was being so polite. This isn't the train station, I told myself, then barged forwards, wedging myself between two big lads.

Monty was stood by the main building. 'In you go, girls.'

Becky and I headed inside, walking down the corridor until we were told to stop. Voices could be heard from one of the rooms ahead.

'… the birds can go in your room.'

'Fuck off!'

There was a roar of laughter from several others.

The voices quietened as we approached the open door. Inside some seven training staff stood around holding metal mugs of tea, dressed in combats and khaki jumpers. One of them, a tubby chap who looked like he'd eaten too many pies, walked across the room, stepped between us and out into the corridor. 'Follow me, ladies.'

I sensed mockery in his voice but didn't dare look at Becky. Instead, I studied him from behind. He had a funny walk, like one leg was shorter than the other.

We were taken to a basement room at the back of the building. It smelt of stale air and looked like a classroom that hadn't been used for ages. It was freezing cold and the only pieces of furniture inside were a few broken chairs and a desk shoved in one corner. I curled up on the floor beside Becky, my bony hip pressing against the hard floor, and tried to get some sleep. I felt cramp in the lower part of my stomach and became worried that I was going to start my period as I hadn't brought sanitary towels. I had overheard some girls talk about going on the pill so that they could control their menstrual cycle during training. I didn't know anything about the pill or any other form of contraception. I didn't know how it was managed in the field. Instead, I repeated the first verse of the Koran in my head and prayed it wouldn't start.

* * *

'Ahmed … AHMED!'

I opened my eyes. Becky was shaking my shoulders roughly. 'Are you OK?'

I sat up and looked around, remembering where I was. 'Yes,' I lied. 'What time is it?'

It was 5 a.m. I must have spoken aloud in my nightmare. I'd dreamt of the forest again, this time running with a pack of soldiers towards a house. I stopped and went inside, where my family were sat around a table eating. I muttered something about being late, but nobody acknowledged me.

Becky got up and started to get dressed. I wanted to ask her about Monty's comment last night or where Adele was but instead I got up and joined her.

An hour later, we headed to the cookhouse. At some

point during the night, other squadrons had joined us because there were about 200 lads in the hall. The recruits were a mixed bunch of former Marines, Paras and even a lad, Sullivan, from the Australian Special Forces, who'd moved to England and had to do it all again here. He was surprisingly small, but a strong chap, with a leg injury that looked like it had been patched up several times. He was well respected amongst the lads and was fascinated with us being here.

The new lads looked up as we walked in; their voices quietened as we weaved through and joined the queue with our mess tins and metal mugs. I didn't feel like eating but would have to force it down because we had a good few hours of training ahead of us. All I kept thinking was where we would sit. Would we be separated? I couldn't bear the idea of sitting around a table of hostility but decided I had to get used to it. I spotted a six-seater table with two empty chairs on the end and signalled to Becky with my eyes. As soon as we sat down, the lads began eating faster, and then all four of them got up and left.

Staff James, the tubby chap from the previous night, appeared at the door. 'Listen in, lads,' he said, putting a hand into his smock pocket and bringing out a large pair of frilly knickers. 'We found these, so if any of you have lost a pair come and claim them later.'

The lads roared with laughter. I didn't understand

the joke and looked round at Becky who was suppressing a smile. 'Make the most it,' she said. 'Nothing gets funny after this.'

After breakfast, we were taken into a theatre to watch a training film. Adele came in just as it came to an end and sat down as the lights came back on.

One of the trainers walked up to the front and switched off the wall screen. He looked like one of my bus drivers from Manchester; a silver fox with a big moustache and a puffy face. His eyes scanned over us like we were leftovers from his takeaway last night.

'OK, lads, hope that's given you enough to think about. Any questions?'

There was a silent reply.

'Right, lads, make your way back to your block.'

The room filled with noise as the boys got up and started heading for the door. Not sure where to go, I looked around for Becky.

'Girls!' Monty walked towards us. 'I want you ready, in sports kit, outside in ten.'

Becky put her hand up.

'Yes, I know about your knee, I spoke to the medic,' Montague cut in. 'You do know that if you can't train after this week, you're off the course?'

Becky nodded frantically in agreement. 'Yeh, sir, I understand.'

He turned to me and Adele. 'You two – in kit.'

Ten minutes later, we were stood outside in sports kit.

It was a cold morning. A couple of lads from regulars walked past and stared at me like I was an alien. I ignored them. I was getting use to these strange looks.

I turned my attention to Adele and studied her legs: strong and muscular. She was also taller than me, which meant her strides would be wider and, of course, she was built like an Amazon, just like the rest of them.

Glumly I looked away and began stretching my legs against a wall. I could only do my best, I thought.

I'd spent all my spare time in the gym getting fit just to keep up with these girls. I hated running and, unfortunately, running played a big part in this training.

I will be miles behind, I thought, and all the trainers will be watching. Then they'll bin me.

Monty came out of the building and pointed to a Jeep parked up the side. 'You two, get in.'

Adele and I jumped into the back while Monty stood talking to Becky, pointing his finger in her face every so often.

'Have you been training?' asked Adele with an authoritarian voice.

'A bit,' I said quietly.

There was a pause, and then I asked, 'Have you?'

'Yes, every day,' she replied.

I looked out of the window, now feeling ten times worse.

Silver Fox got into the front and started up the engine. Monty got into the back with us. 'Where's Taylor?' he asked the driver.

I thought we'd got rid of him at female selection.

'Here he comes.' Silver Fox pointed at Taylor through the windscreen.

To my dismay, Taylor got in with Monty and didn't look at me, though I sensed he acknowledged Adele.

Then we were on our way, driving out of the barracks along a bumpy track.

Monty turned to both of us. 'We're going to do a run to measure your fitness level.' He paused and looked straight at me.

I nodded and felt butterflies in my stomach. I knew what that meant.

Twenty minutes later the vehicle stopped and we all jumped out. Monty didn't waste any time and immediately explained the route: along a track that disappeared into the distance, then apparently there was a canal, then a bridge that would bring us back here.

'I'll give you a moment to stretch.'

A moment really did mean a few seconds and then he had us stand by a small bush at the side of the track, ready to run. My heart was pounding as I stood next to Adele. I tried to concentrate on what was ahead, but her energy was intruding my space.

'Ready ... Go!'

Adele raced ahead. I began running at a pace I could manage, trying not to think about her. Thirty minutes later, we were still running along the gritted track. Adele was getting further and further away, slowly becoming a dot in the distance. I was still running at a steady pace, mesmerised by her figure in front; she had Monty and another trainer running on either side of her, while I had Taylor grunting behind me. I didn't like him and he didn't like me.

I increased my pace a notch to the fastest steady pace I could manage. Time became endless and strange thoughts whizzed through my head; mundane chores that I had to do around London; whether I should stay with the company; the image of my parents sat on my doorstep waiting for me in the cold; the falling out I had with Shazia and my mum's phone message that the marriage bureau had selected a few chaps to see me. I'd hate to think what they were like from the profile I'd written for myself.

I pushed these thoughts to one side and tried to focus on the present moment. Suddenly I realised I was half-way along the canal and could clearly see Adele in front.

'Go on, Ahmed, get in front of her.' Taylor's voice was close to my left ear. 'Go on, just run in front.' I didn't know what else to do but take his order.

I gasped for air and widened my stride, quickening my pace at the same time until I was just behind Monty, who looked round and didn't even attempt to hide his shock as he let me through to overtake Adele on the narrow pathway of the canal.

My legs became numb as I ran a few metres past her.

'Now slow down and set your pace,' Taylor said, still running behind me. I did as I was told.

'Come on, keep going.' Monty was now on my other side.

I could feel my body waking up to another level, boosted by an adrenalin rush from the verbal support I'd never had before. Ten minutes later, we were heading towards a bridge.

'Now give it all you can, Ahmed, to the bridge.' Monty's lanky figure hovered over me. Though I was clearly in front of Adele, they continued to push me to my limit.

I sped up, focused on the bridge, and ran as fast as I could. No longer could I feel my feet on the ground and nothing else mattered as I reached the end. But when I did, my legs couldn't stop going for some bizarre reason. I panicked.

'Keep running!' Taylor could see what was happening.

'Slow down to the other side of the bridge and come back.'

Thankfully, my legs slowed down as I came back, but the coughing and spluttering were uncontrollable.

Adele slowly ran to the finish line and then began limping. I put my hand out to her. She paused, looked at me and then shook it.

'Sir, I think I've sprained my ankle.' Adele stood in front of Montague.

'OK, we'll see a medic when we get back.' He turned to me. 'Any injuries, Ahmed?'

'No, sir,' I replied.

Adele and I walked back to the Jeep.

'What happened to your ankle?' I asked her.

'Just went down on it,' she replied dismissively.

I felt both amazed and bad about the outcome of the run. It meant nothing to me except personal achievement, but to Adele it was losing face in front of the army; being beaten by a civvy.

Twenty minutes later, I was stood at the start line of the assault course with my helmet on. Half of the recruits had been taken off to do another exercise, including Adele and Becky.

A trainer demonstrated the safety instructions; balancing along narrow poles elevated twenty feet off the ground, climbing up widely spaced bars and jumping off at ridiculous heights. He was small, agile and had a body like a boy. He made it look easy, though my stomach churned just watching.

The assault course is used to teach us techniques for crossing rough terrain and to familiarise us with tactical movements encountered during combat. Pirbright was known to hold the toughest assault course of all the military barracks.

'Get to the front, midget!' Staff Phillips growled at me from behind. I dived forward, pushing through the lads, and scrambled to the front.

I'd first noticed Staff Phillips this morning, hovering at the back of the theatre when we were watching the film. He appeared to be in his late forties with a shaven head that created a green curvy shape where his hairline receded. There were very few here who wore glasses, but his were jam jars, making his eyes look massive. To complicate matters, he was a bit cock-eyed so I had no idea who he was looking at.

When the demonstration was over, the staff put us in teams. My name was called out to join the second group. I walked over to them and I heard a few tuts from the lads. I tried to ignore them but knew they saw me as a hindrance; one man down.

'OK, lads, on your marks…' A gun was fired and the first team were off.

There was lots of shouting; the trainers hurling abuse, the lads cheering their mates on. I just stared in amazement. I had never seen such powerful body action in all my life, effortlessly splurging aggression and adrenalin. Physically, it goes without saying, they were built bigger and stronger. It was only now that I realised why men were better suited to the frontline than women.

The lads finished more or less at the same time, their faces were red and sweat was pouring down from inside their helmets.

Staff Phillips walked over to our group. 'OK, lads, team effort.' He looked at me stood in the middle of the giants. 'Ahmed, you go first.'

My head began to spin at his unexpected order and could feel the breakfast travelling up from my stomach.

'On your marks...'

The gun fired before I had a chance to think.

Eyes wide, I charged up the wooden plank, slowly building speed and momentum, then leapt up onto a pole. Somehow I stayed on but my balance was all over the place because of the webbing (the belt kit which held my ammo, water bottle and other kit in pouches) around my waist. I looked down and was horrified to see Staff Taylor walking alongside. He shouted at me to speed up, but as I jumped to the next pole, my foot didn't reach far enough and I fell between the wide gap onto the ground.

'Get back up there!' Taylor hissed, now stood above me. I heard the gun fire again and looked round. To my horror, the rest of my team were charging towards me. I knew if I didn't move out of the way, I would be flattened.

I rolled to one side just as they passed, then I ran back to the start line to take the poles once again. This time I ran faster up the rank and managed to stay on, but when I got to the end of the last pole, I froze with fear at the twenty-foot drop.

'Ahmed! Jump! Now!' Taylor was not leaving my side.

No. I felt sick and wanted to climb down instead.

'Now!'

I closed my eyes and jumped, landing on my feet on the soft ground but then fell backwards onto my bum.

'Get up!' He screamed, his face the colour of a fire extinguisher.

I scurried over to the ten-foot wall and took a jump, clamping my arms over the top as my feet were scrambling below. My arms weren't strong enough, though, and I slid back down. I took another run at it, bashing my knees against the wall as I jumped up, but my arms were now throbbing, giving way and making me drop down. I closed my eyes in defeat. I didn't want to go back and try again – I knew my arms couldn't take it.

'You! Help her over.' Taylor ordered a lad stood on the sideline.

Within seconds, a pair of hands clamped round my ankles and flung me over the wall. Unfortunately, the recruit overestimated my weight and I went flying up like a rocket through the air and landed quite a bit away from the wall on the other side.

'I said give her a leg up, not throw her over. Stupid twit!'

I got dizzy as I stood up, straightened my webbing, which had crawled up to my ribcage, then charged under the barbed wire, dragging my body through. I wanted to stop and have a rest but couldn't. I came out the other end and tried to stand up, but fell back down as my webbing pouch got caught in the wire.

'Get out of there, Ahmed!' someone screamed from a distance.

Off I ran to the twenty-foot bars. I clambered up, kicking out as high as I could because the space between each one was too wide for my legs and my hands could hardly grip the bars properly. Suddenly my foot slipped, causing me to flip backwards, suspended by one leg hooked over a bar. I gasped. My eyes dropped down to two upside-down trainers, waving their arms at me.

'What are you doing up there? This isn't a circus!'

I felt my leg slipping and panicked as I tried to swing back up to catch the bar above. My stomach muscles hurt but I didn't care, I was about to fall and land on my head.

I finally got down the other side of the bars, where Taylor was waiting for me at the last exercise, the water crossing.

'Move it!' he said, handing me the swing rope.

The rope was so thick I could hardly get my fingers around it. Ready to swing, I looked down and froze at the massive drop I had to cross, which was even bigger than that between the poles.

'Don't think, Ahmed,' Taylor's low, threatening voice was millimetres away from my left ear.

Somehow I tore my eyes away and swung forwards, but let go too soon, causing my body to fly through the air and then drop into the trough of water. It felt like I was drowning. I panicked and splashed around frantically before standing up and realising that the water only came to my waist.

I stood to attention afterwards with my team, ready to be debriefed. I was drenched, my head was burning beneath the helmet, which we weren't allowed to take off, and, from their silence, sensed a damning judgement amongst the recruits like I was wasting the regiment's time.

Staff Phillips walked over to the other teams. 'Good effort, lads,' he began, 'but I don't think you were getting through fast enough…' He talked them through his critical analysis, pointing out what each lad was doing wrong and where.

Then he turned to us. 'As for you lot … you were shit!'

I stared bleakly at the treetops in the distance. This was worse than the last eight weeks of female selection put together and we weren't even through the morning yet. My body felt it had been kicked a thousand times and I missed Liz.

Phillips pointed at me. 'Where was she when you lot were all at the finish line?'

I didn't like the way this was going.

'The fastest out of you lot should have been helping the others get through. You get nothing until the last man is in.' He was now shouting. 'You will do it again!'

I couldn't believe my ears. No. Not again. Please! I was just coming to terms with almost dying up there. I couldn't take another bashing.

Mortified, I walked back to the start line with my team.

'On your marks…'

The gun fired and we were off again. This time, two lads stayed behind me all the way, aggressively pushing me through each obstacle like a rag doll. Over the wall they threw me and I was kicked in the face by one of the lads in front. I thought my head was going to come off; the side of my face burned like hell from his boot; I couldn't see properly in one eye and tasted blood inside my mouth. Before I could think too much about it, I was dragged under the barbed wire from both sides, then pushed up the bars where I'd done the circus act. The heights felt higher this time, but this was the least of my worries when I was thrown into the tunnel. Last time I was alone and crawled through fast because of my size, though it severely bruised my elbows and knees. This time I was sandwiched between two lads as I scrambled through on all fours, then the lad in front suddenly stopped in the darkness. Nobody moved. I closed my eyes and prayed he moved soon before I screamed. The air became thin and made me feel claustrophobic. I couldn't breathe, move or see, and the side of my face was still throbbing. I wondered if this was being done deliberately by someone outside.

After what felt like an eternity, the lad finally moved. I crawled forwards as fast as I could, my face in his arse, my knees taking a hammering on the concrete, and squinted up at the first slit of light. I took a deep breath as soon as his arse was out of the way and filled my lungs. It was an amazing feeling, but it didn't last as I was pulled over the scramble nets and then dragged to the finish line.

Relieved to be in one piece, I took my flask out of my daysack and threw the cold water over my face. I wanted to sit down and rest but there was no time.

Staff James took us over to our next exercise.

'Same teams, lads,' he ordered. 'First group, stay here, the rest of you fuck off over there and do some press-ups.'

Staff James disappeared off with the other group. We got down and started pumping.

Digsby, one of the lads from my squadron, was beside me. He reminded me of the Milkybar Kid, but twenty years on with a nose that looked like it had been punched a few times.

'What I want to know,' he said breathlessly, 'is what you girls are doing on our course.'

I kept my head down, just focusing on the press-ups.

'She's not allowed to say?' another probed.

'Mate, she's gonna have to kill us if she does.' Someone else piped up, followed by strenuous laughter.

'Which unit you from, Ahmed?' Digsby wasn't giving up.

I kept quiet, wanting the other team to come back so I could stop these press-ups. They could interrogate me all they wanted – they wouldn't get anything out of me.

'They're back, lads.'

Heads down, we began pumping faster.

'Oi! What do you call that?' Staff James's voice could be heard in the distance 'You! Another ten.'

I lunged down and up, strands of hair fell over my face from the helmet, which lay heavy on my head.

'Right, you lot follow me. Ahmed – do the other eighty later.'

I stood up, wiped the grit from the heel of my hands and followed Staff James. The other team passed us; helmets in hands, glazed expressions, red faces dripping with sweat.

Around the corner, Staff James pointed to a Jeep parked at the bottom of a steep slope. 'Pretty straightforward, lads, all you have to do is get it to the top. You've got two minutes to come up with a plan. When I call, your time starts.'

We all turned in to one another and began talking simultaneously. One of the lads suggested I get into the driver's seat and steer the vehicle. We all thought it was a good idea.

All too soon, Staff James was back. There was no plan.

We ran to the Jeep and to our dismay two trainers were sat in the front, leisurely talking to one other. They were built like brick houses, adding another ton of weight to the vehicle. I squeezed between two lads at the back and placed my palms flat on the bumper.

We pushed, but it wasn't moving. The lads roared.

'Come on, lads! Move the fucker!' shouted Sullivan, the Australian ex-Special Forces, taking the lead.

The sun was beating down on us and like slaves we pushed, until finally it moved an inch. The shouting got louder, sweat poured down our faces.

'Come on!' I heard myself shout, but couldn't bring myself to swear. Our momentum got the vehicle creeping up. I couldn't help thinking this team was one man down because my strength didn't match that of a man. Halfway up, the vehicle suddenly stopped and began rolling backwards. The roars got louder. I moved my hands down to the grill, my lower back stabbing with pain. Meanwhile the trainers sat in the front and continued their leisurely chitchat.

'Don't lose it!' Sullivan shouted. 'Up! Up! Up!'

We had to get this vehicle to the top otherwise we'd all be thrown off the course. I couldn't face being the cause of that. Suddenly my hand slipped, causing me to fall to the ground. The vehicle continued rolling backwards. The shouting got louder. I looked up, inches away from being trapped beneath one of the wheels. A rough hand suddenly grabbed me by the collar and threw me back onto the vehicle, bashing my forehead.

'We're losing it, lads! Push! Push!'

The roars continued. Another surge of adrenalin and

the vehicle began moving the other way. The grill was cutting into my hands but I just had to keep going.

'Come on! Beeeeeautiful! Up! Up!' Sullivan aggressively sung the motivation.

Eventually the vehicle came away from us and rolled down the other side of the hill. The feeling was unbelievable and I was overwhelmed with emotion. We cheered, grabbed each other to almost a hug then began chasing after the vehicle for some reason.

One of the trainers poked his head out of the vehicle, not quite believing what he was seeing. 'Get back up there, you fucking morons!' he shouted. 'This isn't a game show!'

* * *

Staff Phillips paced between the ranks as we stood on last parade, his presence sending terror amongst us. He looked really cheesed off.

'Listen, lads, if you want ten out of ten and a little red star for pushing a fucking mini over a hump you're wasting my time. I don't care about yours. That was a fucking disgrace up there. Half of you almost became rations packs, and we're not even on the hills yet!'

I stared ahead in blank exhaustion. The stinging around my waist where the webbing had rubbed intensified. I tried to figure out who saved me from being squashed under the Jeep. Couldn't have been Digsby – he wouldn't have noticed – or Sullivan, because he was doing all the shouting when I went down.

'Forget the TA. This is 21 SAS.' Phillips skimmed the front rank. 'I want speed and aggression. I want to see you move on those hills.'

Just at that moment, the other team appeared and quickly joined our ranks. Staff Taylor was leading them, his face like thunder.

'Fuckin' sloppy the lot of you!' He joined Staff Phillips at the front. 'We will run over tough terrain day and night carrying forty, fifty pounds on our backs. Any wasters can piss off now!' His scream echoed around the deserted barrack grounds, creating an eerie silence afterwards.

Phillips crunched off the gravel, waving a dismissive hand at us. 'Go on, piss off, the lot of you.'

Relieved by his order, we walked back to our kit that was piled high on the track beside the jerry cans (large plastic containers holding water for refilling our water bottles).

I scratched a film of filth off my forehead and hobbled over. I yanked my Bergen out from the bottom of the pile and dragged it towards a four-ton truck parked on the lay-by, wondering what the hell I was I doing here.

'AHMED!'

I swung round at the sound of Taylor's voice and then searched for him amongst the recruits coming towards me.

'Pick your fuckin' handbag up, you stupid bird!'

Frantically I slung the Bergen onto my back and bombed it, my webbing furiously swinging around my hips. Tears sprang to my eyes, making my vision blurred as I dodged a tree line of low branches that almost took my eyes out, then scurried down a grassy bank. My breathing was heavy – coming in sharp bursts, heart-attack style. My hip was also playing up, causing me to grind to a halt. Body folded over, I opened my mouth to heave something up but nothing came out.

'While you're down there do the eighty.' Phillips came up behind me.

I fell to my bony knees, the cold digging into the heels of my hands. One … two… But it was too much with the belt kit, and I crashed down on my face. I stared at a blade of grass sprinkled with dew. The smell of fresh dirt was strong.

I prised my face off the ground as Phillips walked off, then staggered to the vehicle where most of the recruits were now inside.

I stepped up, grabbed the steel bars and then tipped the Bergen inside, but didn't have the energy to get myself over. Chin hooked over the tailgate and blinded by wisps of hair, I heaved my body up but my foot missed the metal ledge for a third time. Worried by how close behind Phillips was, I prayed, not just to Allah but to all the gods.

Inside, the recruits watched anxiously. Sullivan stepped forward but stayed low so as not to be seen from outside. He dragged my Bergen to where his was placed then gave me his hand. Before I could reach for it, my body toppled over and hit the floor with a thud, shattering the silence inside. Nobody moved.

'Ahmed,' Sullivan whispered.

I spun round and stared into his green eyes, then followed his gaze down to my webbing where a pouch had come unfastened and everything was hanging out. Frantically, I began thumping everything back in with my bruised knuckles. Meanwhile the rest of the recruits clambered in, pushing themselves into the left-over spaces. Digsby aggressively squeezed his Bergen on the other side of mine, passing a wink in my direction.

'That last bit was murder!' Digsby said, levelling up with Sullivan's glare above me as I sat between them in a daze. 'If someone had asked me my name or where I lived I would've have had no idea.'

The truck started up with a jerk, tossing me onto Digsby's smock. I pushed myself off and began coughing as a black cloud of fumes rose through the canvas flap.

'I can't get my head around you two.' Digsby pointed at Becky then me. 'You could be home baking cupcakes.'

No one laughed, no one cared.

I tilted my head back and closed my eyes, feeling the blisters set my feet on fire.

It's only pain, I told myself, only pain.

CHAPTER EIGHT

THE HILLS

THE FIRST EVENING we joined the lads for the hills phase, they were already stood in rank in the courtyard at the Chelsea Barracks. The numbers had gone down to 100 or so men and a couple of new faces were doing the hills phase again. Becky and I put our Bergens down in front of us and stood to attention. Adele hadn't turned up, thank God, and finally my security clearance had come through.

I should have been ecstatic about it but everything else in my life was going from bad to worse. Mum and Dad weren't speaking to me. I didn't blame them after my desertion when they came down to visit. I had got back to my flat and they had left a carrier bag of food outside my front door. I broke down in floods of tears; partly from the relief of getting through another arduous weekend of training but also because I felt terrible about my bad behaviour in the face of their good intentions. I phoned them straight away. Dad answered and when he heard my voice called Mum, which was normal, but this time I didn't want it. I pleaded with him, telling him how sorry I was for not being home and asking whether they received my message and where they had stayed, but I knew they had ended up with the Croydon family. I tried to rescue the conversation by asking how the family was, which sounded odd as I had never asked about them before. Dad didn't respond and instead handed the phone to Mum, which made it worse. I took a deep breath. Her voice became like one of those VHS tapes on fast-forward: it just went on and on saying how shameful it was for them not to be able to stay with their daughter. I tried to interrupt, apologising profusely, but it didn't make any difference. A part of me wanted to put the phone down, but I knew this would only fuel the situation.

We had been issued extra kit for the hills and could feel the difference in weight. Three new trainers stood at the front of the ranks talking to the recruits. Briggs was the main man and stood in the middle. He was short, with a strong Liverpudlian accent, shaven head, very pale skin and light grey eyes. He noticed our movement in the back.

'Who are you?' he asked in a high-pitched voice, almost like a girl.

Thankfully, Becky did the honours. 'Sir, we were asked to join selection,' she announced proudly ... too proudly.

Briggs spun round to the other staff stood on either side of him, both towering over him. 'Who said?'

One of them stepped forward and whispered something in his ear.

I saw Briggs's eyes widen, then he exploded. 'What the fuck? What the *fuck*?'

With that, he stormed off into the main building behind us.

Oh my ... the colonel hadn't even told him!

I kept my gaze fixed in the gap Briggs had left between the other two trainers, my hands clenched tight behind my back. Minutes later, he was back, his face like thunder. I had never been so scared in my life.

'Get your fuckin' crap hats on!' he screamed at us. 'You're not in the unit yet.'

Becky and I looked at each other and suddenly realised we were wearing berets, the ones issued to admin people. All the other lads wore a khaki woolly hat. I had no idea what a crap hat was or why they were called that – but began rummaging through my Bergen for something that looked green and woolly. Finally, Becky brought out a balaclava that I guessed the lads had rolled up into a hat. I delved deeper into my Bergen to find mine. My hands were shaking as I put it on.

'Who the fuck do you think you are?' he snarled, then turned back to the lads and carried on giving the orders.

I could feel my face burning; not through humiliation, that feeling had gone a long time ago, but the thought of having him as my trainer for the many months ahead.

The challenge on selection was no longer purely physical. We also had to learn to read a map. If you couldn't work out the best route from A to B in the quickest time, it didn't matter how fast you could run. A lot of the recruits, if not all, had been on trekking expeditions before. I didn't even know which way to hold a map let alone relate contour lines to terrain or read a compass. How foolish of me to think the worst was over after the assault course.

The journey down to Wales usually took around five hours, sometimes more, depending on the traffic. Some of the lads would sleep straight through but I couldn't. I would look out of the window at the cars, my weapon squeezed between my knees. Becky and I always sat separately and there would always be an empty seat next to me until the coach was full.

On the way down, we would pick up 'C' squadron in Bramley, 'E' Squadron would already be in the Brecon Beacons as they were based in Wales. The bus would stop a mile away from our basha area, our camp at the bottom of a steep hill. Staff would bang on the sides of the vehicle to shake us back to reality. It was cruel. Drowsy and with our eyes still adjusting to the darkness, we got out as quickly as possible into the cold. Blindly we'd search through the Bergens being thrown out by the lads in front. The one labelled 'Ahmed' would always be last.

The first time I tried to put the Bergen on my back, it was too heavy to sling over my shoulder and when I did eventually get it on, I couldn't reach down and pick up my weapon laid over my right boot. This isn't working, I thought. If I wriggled the tips of my fingers forward to touch the weapon, the Bergen slid towards my head. How the hell was I going to do the training if I couldn't even carry the Bergen?

By the time I had mastered it and stood up, everyone had disappeared, including the bus. I looked around in a panic and then just caught a head torch disappear around the corner into the darkness. Quickly I moved forward, feeling a blunt pain shoot down the back of my knees. But I had to keep going otherwise I'd lose them.

It took thirty long minutes to get where the rest of the recruits had already bashered up (set up shelter) and were getting ready to sleep. I dropped my Bergen and pulled out the poncho. Using a pen torch as an aid, I spread the sheet of waterproof flat out on the ground, suspended its corners around a tree trunk with paracord and elastic bungees, then stabbed a couple of metal pegs into the ground to hold it down.

'Ahmed.' Digsby approached me holding a notebook. 'You're on stag at zero three hundred hours.'

I nodded and crawled into my sleeping bag under the poncho. Standing guard, keeping a watch for the enemy, in the middle of the night, meant no sleep. By the time you close your eyes it's time to get up, then after the watch, when you're about to doze off, its reveille, a signal to get up and start training. I curled up like an embryo in the sleeping bag. It was so thin, I could feel the uneven frosty ground pressing against my skin. A twig poked the side of my stomach but I was too tired to pull it out and didn't want to risk the poncho collapsing on top of me. The wildlife kept me awake and the cold wouldn't leave my bones. I was anxious about the training. All I knew was that we had an eight-mile run before breakfast, in army boots.

I slept with my weapon by my side. We had to take it everywhere with us no matter what we were doing, be it sleeping, toilet or training. If we were caught without it, we were off the course.

I said my prayers to Allah, asking for strength to get me through the training and tried to sleep. The woods were still. I could hear snoring. My eyelids became heavy and finally I was drifting off.

'Ahmed.'

I felt a kick in the ribs, then heard a recruit crunch off back to his sleeping bag. I opened my eyes and suddenly realised where I was and that it must be my turn for stag. Frantically, I scrambled out of my sleeping bag, the sharp air shaking off my drowsiness, then headed to the mouth of the woods. It was freezing. I was breathing puffy clouds. I rubbed my hands and began to pace up and down, keeping guard of the basha area. The hour went very slowly. I didn't know what to do with myself. It was boring and I had to stay awake.

I thought back to our colonel. He was a man of honour and he treated the officers and privates at the barracks alike. The recruits were a mixture of bankers, lawyers and surgeons, but this meant nothing to him – we were all equal and classless and all had a job to do. Also, I liked that the regiment's success was not measured on financial profit, as success is in the corporate world, nor did the recruits get worked up about how much someone else was being paid. People's mindsets here were focused on the bigger picture, the team spirit created by the bond of our uniforms.

Daylight broke, the birds twittered in the trees and I headed back to my sleeping bag after stag. My battle with the cold continued to keep me awake. The lads started rustling around me, heading to the woods for a wee. It was 5 a.m. I unzipped the sleeping bag and struggled out, throwing the poncho to one side, which had collapsed on top of me.

The training began with the eight-mile run. My feet were still recovering from the training back at the barracks, the skin on the back of my heels raw.

I arrived last and joined the recruits who were sorting their breakfast out. *I must eat*, I told myself, rummaging through my Bergen. I had been given pork rations for breakfast but wasn't allowed to eat them because of my religion. I'd had endless debates with friends in the past who would argue that pigs were in fact very clean animals and that by eating their own waste they should be seen as inherently self-contained and tidy. There was also the view that eating pork was only forbidden in Islam because pigs were difficult to raise in hot countries as they needed to drink a lot of water to survive. Then there was Jinnah, the Muslim idol who fought for Pakistan's independence in 1947, who ate pork and drank alcohol. I once made the grave mistake of raising

Jinnah with Dad as well as questioning whether Muslims would be allowed to have heart transplants from pigs if it was a matter of life and death. He looked away, trying to think of an answer, but I never got one.

I watched the recruits from under a tree as I forced a cheese and onion sandwich down. I'd sneaked it into my Bergen back at the barracks when we were packing for the training. It was squashed because I had stupidly put it at the bottom and piled everything on top. It tasted sickly from the mayo and I could feel it heaving back up. I tried to keep it down by swigging cold water from my flask, which dribbled down my neck, sending a chill all over. I could taste the strong onions on my tongue mushed into the slimy texture. Why don't I go and join them out there? They won't tell the staff I was eating a sandwich instead of my pork sausage breakfast ration. But I was scared in case one of them did. I didn't want to stand out or give them an excuse to get rid of me. I watched them light up the hexi burners and start cooking. I had never been on the hills, never been in the Girl Guides or slept outside as a kid. This whole world was alien to me. Everything was a struggle and I didn't know how I was going to get through the morning, let alone the weekend.

Parade was at 6.55 a.m. for a 7 a.m. start. It was 6.50 a.m. and I was still stuffing my sleeping bag in my Bergen. I fought back the tears. Everything fitted fine before leaving the barracks. Becky offered to help but had to leave or else she too would get in trouble. I finally arrived on parade three minutes late and stood to attention at the back, wriggling my toes around in my soggy socks.

'Ahmed, what time is parade?' Briggs asked.

'6.55, sir.' I replied quietly.

'And what time is it now?'

'6.58, sir.'

He didn't have to say any more, it was a given. I dropped to my hands and knees, with the Bergen still on my back, and started the press-ups with everyone around, still stood to attention. The shooting pains were back and my feet were stinging.

'What do you call them?!' Briggs screamed. 'Take your fat arse and start running and don't stop till I tell you.'

I looked up at him from the press-up position, not because he said I had a fat arse. I followed his finger over to some foggy hills in the distance then got up and ran after it, kicking up clumps of sheep manure on the way. Before I knew it, the rest of the recruits were behind me and then overtaking.

We were all now heading to our first rendezvous point (RV) across the mountainous terrain to practise using a compass and reading a map. I'd never seen an

Ordnance Survey map before, never held a compass and had no idea how to use them. My pace of learning was much slower than the rest of them, who had trained in the outdoors for many years.

Later we navigated with a map and grid references. We crossed a number of checkpoints, at each of which we were given another six-figure grid reference to memorise and get to. There was no knowing when the last checkpoint would be. Sometimes the terrain would be marshy and come up to my waist, at which point I'd get worried that if I carried on it would swallow me up like quicksand and nobody would ever find me again. The river crossing was pretty lethal, too, especially if you dropped your Bergen in the water – you might as well go home if that happened.

My shoulders burned the first time I took off the Bergen. I could feel the rawness tingling beneath the cold material from the straps rubbing over a 48-hour period. At first I tried sticking plasters on my shoulders, but they just peeled off within seconds. Then I tried bandaging my shoulders up, which made me look like the Michelin man and I was unable to move my arms around. Finally, I had no choice but to try to cushion the straps in some way; a couple of sanitary towels felt-tipped in green ink and stuck on the inside of the straps did the trick.

One thing I didn't consider on the hills was the strong wind. It scared the hell out of me when I walked along the edges of mountains and cliffs. I worried that the wind would tilt my Bergen the wrong way, and being so light I would follow it down into a valley.

By the end of the weekend, I was a broken woman. The journey back to London was quiet in the coach; we were all too exhausted to speak. Not to mention we had a lot to do when we got back, including 'sort our shit out', as Briggs put it. That meant cleaning our weapons, which took ages. My weapon always seemed to be the muddiest, because I had used it as a walking stick when my legs were about to give way going up a mountain, but never in front of a trainer.

Our coach driver looked like Les Dawson with a white shirt pulled over his big belly. He had faded green tattoos on both arms and would stand outside his vehicle watching the muddy uniforms walking towards him, then refuse us entry until we changed into dry kit.

'Ahmed! Both your legs are the same size as one of my six-year-old daughter's!' Briggs shouted as we got changed by the motorway lay-by. A cackle of laughter followed from the other trainers but I wasn't fazed, just relieved he didn't comment on my hairy legs. The coach would carry a terrible whiff from the lads. I don't know what they put in these ration packs but these guys stank.

I stared out of the window at traffic passing on the motorway and let my mind wander because I couldn't sleep. Training with the lads wasn't easy, especially the Welsh ones from 'E' Squadron. Their faces blurred into one another except for one in particular who stuck in my head. I didn't know his name but he was tall, had a freckled nose and such a strong Welsh accent I could hardly understand him. Every time the training staff was around, he would make condescending remarks about me, a bit like Adele had on female selection.

I was desperate to hear a familiar voice when we got back and called home from the changing rooms at the barracks. Dad answered the phone. I was expecting Mum. A blanket of silence hung between us. I tried to think of something to say but nothing came to mind. The full magnitude of how much our relationship had deteriorated suddenly sank in. There is nothing to discuss, I realised, because we don't talk. It had been fifteen years since we shared a game of chess and our relationship had become even more distant since I moved away. I wanted to understand my father's time in the army. Having now read up on the partition of India and Pakistan I appreciated the colossal extent of life's harsh experiences he must have gone through, along with many others. I thought back to my teenage years; living in a warm house, with two meals a day and surrounded by family.

A far cry from what I assumed his life in the army was like, not knowing if he would live to see another day.

The phone was suddenly passed to Mum and within seconds she was off, telling me all about their plans to go to hajj. I stopped listening and just kept thinking of Dad. It felt like something had died inside of him – hope. Hope that I would return home from the horror image of me living in a bedsit or shacked up with a lad. How demoralised I must have made him feel when I walked out that day, yet he never said anything. How crushing that must have been.

'Are you fasting?' Mum asked me sharply.

'Yes,' I lied; I'd completely forgotten it was the month of Ramadan.

I held my breath for another dose of accusations then heard my nephew's baby voice in the background. I felt a pang of jealousy that my sister was there and not me and also guilty because I couldn't remember the last time I'd called my sister. But she could call me, I told myself. She did, I suddenly remembered, several times, and left voice messages, but I didn't get round to calling back because I was so wrapped up in myself.

I tried to rescue the conversation by telling Mum I was terribly sorry for not visiting and calling more often but my apology fell on deaf ears. I put the phone away, composed a calm exterior, then went back out to the courtyard where the lads were cleaning their weapons. Inside I was screaming. I didn't understand what I was doing any more, why I was still here, why I wanted to finish or where I would go next.

*   *   *

'Ahmed, where's your weapon?'
    I looked around at Lewis as I loaded up the truck. He was a small, stocky recruit who looked like one of those photo-fit profiles on a murder investigation TV series. His accent was northern, I guessed Yorkshire. But I didn't want to ask in case I'd have to confess to being a Lancashire girl and causing a Wars of the Roses scenario.

    'Here,' I replied, pointing down to where it lay across my left boot.

    'Is it OK if I leave my weapon with you for a few minutes?' he asked, walking over as if he had already made up his mind. He hardly acknowledged me as he placed it down and disappeared out of the shelter.

    I pulled the canvas around the vehicle, tying it securely in the corners. I wasn't feeling so good, having cramp in my lower stomach. We were heading to the Brecons again for 'VW Valley' weekend, a tough run along the old road and summiting Cefn-Y-Bryn. I realised later that VW stood for Voluntary Withdrawal – which was what most recruits did on this weekend. I packed strong painkillers, anti-inflammatory cream, bandages and of a tub of Vaseline (which meant more to me than my ration packs).

'Ahmed! Why have you got two weapons?'

I spun round at Briggs's voice. Lewis was nowhere to be seen. Lame excuses raced through my mind. If I say one of them belongs to Lewis, I'll get him in trouble and if I say I don't know I will be in even more trouble.

But it was too late. Lewis suddenly reappeared and stopped dead in his tracks as he captured the scene.

*   *   *

'Sorry, Ahmed.'

Minutes later, Lewis and I were both stood on the racetrack at the barracks holding our weapons above our head, arms locked. The rest of the group were in the vehicle parked in the courtyard, watching. The heavens cracked open and it lashed down. Within seconds my khaki T-shirt was soaked to the skin. This was not a good start.

'Right, you fuckin' idiots,' Briggs shouted through the rain, marching towards us. 'This is what happens when you don't have your weapon.'

We began running around the track after him – his pace quickened. Within seconds, my arms started burning. The weapon was heavy and awkward. My arms began to come down.

'Get that weapon back up and move your fuckin' arse, Ahmed!' He was now alongside us. 'Up, up!'

I jolted my arms back up, causing a knee to buckle and send me flying forwards, almost dropping the weapon. I regained balance before falling flat on my face.

'Are you going to do it again?!' he hissed.

'No, sir,' we said in unison.

'What?'

'No, sir!' we shouted.

I tried to think of something to take my mind off the pain but nothing came to mind. This was torture.

Afterwards we jogged back to the glowing headlights of the vehicle and got inside. I crawled to an empty seat. Everyone was watching us. I sat down and began rummaging through my Bergen. Tears sprang to my eyes. The cramp in my lower stomach was getting worse.

No, not now! Please! My periods had become irregular since training. I got anxious, began frantically counting and recounting the days, then forgot when my last one was.

Hot tears flowed down my cheeks. I kept my head down to avoid anyone seeing them. Finally, I found a

T-shirt in my bag, quickly wiped my face and arms with it and then stared out of the window as the vehicle made its way out of London.

The next morning, Becky and I had to set off three hours before the lads because we had to cover the same ground but wouldn't do it in the same time as them.

Several hours later, I was cold, soggy and tired. Becky and the rest of them were nowhere to be seen. I wanted to drop to my knees and cry out like a baby. I was last again. I'd been tabbing, fast walking, alone for hours, keeping my energy up with peanuts and chocolate. My stomach felt acidic. My body was killing me from the weight of the Bergen, webbing and weapon. I'd just left the third RV where Staff Jones had given me a six-figure grid reference for the fourth one, which could be anywhere between four and ten miles away. I climbed and climbed the convex mountain but never seemed to get closer to the top.

The conditions took their toll; the weather got progressively worse, and the sleet was now hitting my face horizontally. It felt like I was coming down with hypothermia as my decision-making was becoming affected by the conditions. I couldn't decide which way to go or how the read the map properly. Head down, I skirted around the edge of the mountain. My eyelids became heavy, I felt drowsy but had to fight it off and keep moving. My foot suddenly slipped and the wind that was blowing against me sent my Bergen over the edge. I'd experienced fear before, but this was raw: I was inches away from falling, the edge was taunting me and I was petrified. My logical side knew I should lower my body but the emotional side was giving in and felt too weak to go on. But these thoughts were wrong. If Becky and I didn't survive the hills, it would be hell for our colonel. The MOD would point their finger at him and ask why he allowed girls to train here in the first place. Where were the trainers when Ahmed fell to her death, they would ask, knowing she had no outdoor or military experience?

These terrifying thoughts turned my mindset 180 degrees, giving me a massive adrenalin kick in a matter of nanoseconds. I forced my body down, holding onto the ground for dear life until I had the strength to crawl back away from the edge and wait for the wind to settle before attempting the trail again. Being stationary for too long was a mistake I'd experienced all too often, whether it was while reading a map, eating or going to the toilet. My legs would seize up, sending shooting pains through the most vulnerable parts of my body when I walked again.

I slowed down to snail's pace, just as a local man ran past wearing sportswear and a raincoat. He looked round at me, then stopped a few metres ahead.

'Are you in the SAS?' he asked, squinting through the rain at me. 'I didn't know they had women.'

I pulled the hood of my windproof over my face, hoping he would go away, which he did eventually when I didn't respond.

I plunged down into a valley then stopped to check my bearings. A teardrop fell onto the plastic casing of my compass, washed away by the rain. I couldn't think straight. I had no idea where I was or when I would reach my next RV. It was getting dark and I needed to quicken my pace.

I kept going until I saw a tent in the distance set on a slope, and a few recruits crawling around the steep hillside. I checked my bearings. The contours on the map didn't match my surroundings. It was an RV, but not mine.

I headed towards another steep mountain, first taking a chocolate bar out to give me the rush I needed to climb up. The wind blew fiercely from behind, sending me flat on my face. It took a while to push myself back up, and the chocolate was stuck on my palm. I licked it off and the texture suddenly changed in my mouth and became chewy. I then realised I had put my hands in some sheep dropping and was eating that too. Unfazed, I pressed on, now using my weapon to help me up. Almost twelve hours had passed and the rain hadn't stopped. Another gust of wind hit me from behind, making me stumble to the ground and skid. My knees and elbows stung beneath the material but I had to carry on.

I was at the end of my tether, about to give in, then … I saw my RV.

As I approached, I saw a couple of staff sat inside a Land Rover – no reason why they should get wet. I made it over to one of them, his piercing blue eyes watching me. I thought he was going to shout at me about something but instead he took me by surprise.

'See that miserable git over there…' he pointed at a lad behind me sat by a four-ton truck with one leg suspended over his Bergen. Thankfully it wasn't Sullivan. The staff looked up to the valleys. 'Ahmed, you are going to get up there and get to the end…'

The staff had never said encouraging words like this before. Even if the staff was saying it for effect, it worked like a magical boost of energy. My body woke up. I went over and began climbing again, all the time trying to gauge the enormity of the task, but even then I underestimated it. There was a RV halfway up, where I got a telling off from staff, shouting at me to hurry up as everyone was already back. But I still had a good few hours to go. I tried to speed up but my hip was giving in. I shoved a couple of painkillers down my neck and suddenly found myself crying uncontrollably; pain, anger and frustration rose to the surface and it felt like I was having a meltdown. I cried about this stupid double life I was leading with my family, why I didn't have a best friend any more, why I wasn't in a relationship. These anxieties went round and round in my head as I crossed the dodgy rivers, boggy marshes and rough terrain.

The hours passed until finally I saw a mirage in the distance; the familiar woods where we had started at the crack of dawn this morning, then down below I saw the sheep track where we began the tab, which looked about a mile away.

Oh my God! I'm here! I thought, and I walked as fast as I could towards it.

Time slowed down, another hour passed before I reached the bashas, where the recruits had already eaten and were taking a rest before our night navigation exercise. I could tell from their expressions that I must have looked a sight. My hair was everywhere, there was mud on my face and I was glassy eyed.

My body was in so much pain I couldn't take the Bergen off my shoulders; it was stuck to my back.

The horrible Welsh recruit with the strong Welsh accent was cleaning his weapon. He suddenly got up and walked over to me. He stood inches away, studying my face, then lifted the Bergen off my back and offered me his beaker of hot tea.

'Thank you.' The words choked out. I was over-whelmed by his generosity. All this time I thought he hated me. I had been so wrong.

I placed the beaker down on a dead patch of grass and pulled off my boots and carefully peeled off my socks soaked in blood, feeling them take some of my skin, then let the cold breeze blow between my toes. I'd lost two of my nails, probably inside the socks some-where, and another felt loose. All in all, my feet were in a bad state. I flicked my penknife open and inserted the point into a juicy blister on my big toe. Salty sweat trickled down my face as I focused on the mini opera-tion. Then, with eyes screwed tight, I lifted a piece of skin hanging off the back of my heel and slapped a gen-erous amount of Vaseline onto the pink skin and stuck it back on like a sandwich.

Becky appeared from behind and stood beside me watching what I was doing.

'I ate some sheep poo,' I mumbled.

Becky looked round at me trying not to laugh. 'What?'

'I was licking some chocolate off my hands and its texture was like ... raisins.'

There was a burst of uncontrollable laughter as she

stood up and headed back to her basha. I couldn't see the funny side of it.

My attention turned to a couple of lads talking behind me.

'I had a big argument with my gal,' one of them said. 'She wouldn't stop going on about the washer … the fuckin' washing machine! I can't talk to her.'

'Mate, we're only halfway through…'

I closed my ears to it all and put my boots back on to go for a pee in the woods. I could feel the beginnings of a flu coming on and was dreading the night exercise. The twigs on the ground cracked noisily beneath my boots. I thought about the stream of bad conversation I'd had with my family, and then my thoughts morphed into memories of home as a kid; the smell of stewed chai, daylight hitting the living room, Dad watching the news, the weekend trip to the cash-and-carry, and I never thought I'd hear myself say this, but I missed the kebab shop, the customers, and even that miserable Beardy.

'Ahmed, where's your weapon?'

I spun round. Briggs was stood at a distance looking through the sight ring of his M16 weapon at me.

It didn't make any difference what I said. I should not be without my weapon.

'Right, you fuckin' idiot.' His scream sounded like a woman being strangled. 'Go and find it!'

I scurried back to the basha area weaving through the thick trees, eyes fixated on spots of light glowing from hexi burners.

'Ahmed,' Becky called as I flew past. 'What's happened?'

Blindly I searched around my Bergen for my weapon. 'You don't want to know,' I replied shakily, grabbing my weapon and running back to the woods, where Briggs was still stood looking through his sight ring at me.

'Hold it over your head.'

I gripped the cold metal, held it above me and raced towards him. The punishment was severe – but I deserved it.

CHAPTER NINE

MY NEW BUDDY

'FUCKIN' HELL, LEWIS!'

'Sorry, mate.'

Sullivan walked over to me, his big bushy eyebrows creased on his small forehead.

'Ahmed, you got your cleaning kit around? Lewis lost his weapon and took mine to pass staff camp and slipped near the shithouse.' Sullivan was holding a very muddy weapon.

Parade was in ten minutes. I desperately needed some hot food down me after that beasting from Briggs. I'd been surviving on cold rations because I still hadn't got my head around how to heat up the ration packs.

I stared up at Sullivan, bewildered, not knowing what

to say. I had no idea why he was coming to me. There were plenty of lads around he could ask. Perhaps he wants to get me in trouble, I thought suspiciously, looking around for any staff hovering in the area.

'You alright with that?' He looked down at my hands that were loosely holding the hexi blocks and lighter to create a small fire for my food to cook on.

Before I could say anything, he took them off me and lit up the cubes in small, quick movements. I watched a small fire begin to glow. Then he poured some water into my metal beaker and placed my ration pack inside to heat up.

'Thanks,' I said, reaching into my Bergen and handing him my cleaning kit. I placed another ration in the beaker for him, the sausage one that I was not going to eat anyway.

A recruit walked past and pushed Sullivan playfully over to one side and then carried on walking. Sullivan watched him disappear. 'Can't trust that one,' he said. 'This morning he was creeping around us when we were still asleep and he should have woken us. It was only because I heard a twig snap under his foot that I woke up, bastard.'

I was surprised to hear that. I thought this kind of thing only went on in female selection. I wondered what had happened to all those girls, especially Adele. Though the lads were aloof towards me and Becky, they seemed more pleasant to be around.

He turned back to me. 'And what happened to you this morning, Ahmed? Your poncho was collapsed over you and your socks were hung out to dry.' He began to laugh. 'Didn't anyone tell you to put your socks inside your sleeping bag to dry against the body heat?'

Somehow I found the energy to smile, but couldn't remember. It was hard enough dealing with what was going on in the moment, let alone what happened a few hours ago. Obviously he hadn't heard what just happened with Briggs, otherwise he'd be cracking up by now. I admired his humour but perhaps it was just his way of getting through.

We sat in silence, me watching the water furiously bubble away in the beaker and him cleaning his weapon beside me.

I was relieved to be sat down. Ever since the assault course on pre-selection, my right hip hadn't been the same. I tried to rest it between intervals and didn't want to tell anyone here, especially the medic in case I was dismissed.

'I know I shouldn't be asking you this,' Sullivan took the main pieces of the weapon apart and placed them on the grass on top of his crap hat, 'but how come you two are here?'

He knew I wasn't going to answer.

'You must be mad to do this.'

Perhaps I was mad, I thought, but wasn't he just as mad?

'So, are you Muslim?'

I nodded. With a name like Ahmed, what do you think? I thought. I handed him the sausage ration then opened mine, not quite believing I was finally going to have some proper hot food. I pulled a plastic spoon out of my smock pocket. It was tied to my buttonhole by a piece of string. The rations tasted amazing and I could feel my throat and chest warm up as it slowly slid down.

'Does that mean you have arranged marriages?' He watched me shovel the food down.

I hesitated before answering. Here we go, I thought, he's probably waiting for me to pour out some terrible story about an arranged marriage and how I was forced to run away, the kind you read about in the tabloids. I didn't like him any more. I wanted him to hurry up cleaning his weapon and get lost.

'Not really,' I replied between mouthfuls, only answering because he had warmed my food up, 'but he would have to be someone my parents are happy with.'

'Would he have to be Muslim?'

I scraped the last bits of food from the bottom and decided not to answer. I'm not going to waste my time trying to open up his mind. I have enough things going on, like dealing with Briggs who was now gunning for me. *I will never leave my weapon again*, I thought, remembering his punishment.

But Sullivan wasn't giving up. 'So, does that mean you can't go out with white boys?'

I stopped and looked up at him. We stared at each other for a moment until we were interrupted by Digsby, who came over and looked straight at Sullivan.

'Parade in five, mate,' he said flatly, then shot a glance at me and walked off.

I wondered what that look was for but didn't spend too much time thinking about it.

Sullivan got up and winked at me. 'I'll give you the cleaning kit back later.'

I watched him go off into the distance and then got back to sorting out my kit. I wondered what the lads thought of me and Becky being here. It didn't feel as bad as when we first joined them. Perhaps they were getting used to us, perhaps we had somehow won their respect by still being here, or perhaps they had no choice in the matter and gritted their teeth. I wondered how the staff took it and thought back to the first evening on parade; Briggs's expression when he found out we were joining the lads will haunt me for the rest of my life. Since then Briggs's motto had been to treat us as bad as the lads, as their equals. There was nothing wrong with that, except sometimes I hated being a lad. Then there was Taylor, who was still hovering around since female selection. What was it with him? Did he have a bet on with the rest of the staff to see which week Becky and I would drop out? Perhaps we were their entertainment. I recalled a few occasions when I must have looked a sight coming back from a beasting. The more these thoughts went round in my head the more determined I was not to throw the towel in.

I shoved everything back in the Bergen the best I could and joined the rest of the recruits in rank. The hot food was now digesting in my stomach and making me sleepy.

Becky was stood at the front next to Sullivan. I wondered if she was managing as well as she seemed to be or breaking inside like me. We still hadn't got to speak much but she seemed to be getting on better with the lads.

Briggs was stood at the front, debriefing us on today's exercise. As always, he was very encouraging. 'Even a one-legged geriatric could have done better than you lot today. What do you think this is? The fucking Ramblers!?' His head was shaking with rage as he paced up and down the front rank, fists clenched tight. 'If you get blisters, so fuckin' what?'

Being small had its advantage amongst these tall lads. I felt desperately tired and closed my eyes for a second and immediately felt my body relax. My mind quickly fought back, freaked out by how close I'd come to dozing off. The repercussions were not worth thinking about.

Briggs dismissed us – 'Piss off.' I needed the toilet before preparing for the night patrol. Through the woods I trod to find a hidden spot. I pulled my pants down and squatted, staring up at the clear sky and focusing on the shiniest star. I thought back to Sullivan. A part of me wanted to find out more about Sullivan without asking him, but I couldn't speak to Becky as I didn't know her that well. I wondered what my parents' reaction would be if I went home with a boy from the army? I knew the answer of course: they'd kill me if I went home with a boy, let alone someone from the army. Then I pondered what life would be like if I had taken the Shazia route. But that would never happen, I told myself. Manchester was where I had always been 'meant' to be, the army was my choice. I suddenly realised that Dad and I were in the same army but fifty years apart – how strange was that? I imagined him dressed in khakis and wondered what wars he was involved in. Syria, Malaya … Burma?

*   *   *

Briggs gathered us under a shelter around a makeshift table with a map spread across it. 'Listen in, lads; you will be dropped off within this area here. Enemy targets are here, here and here…'

I forced my eyes open, trying to focus on the blade of grass Briggs was pointing with on the map. Night exercises were a killer. Not only did it take twice as long to navigate in the dark but it was twice as dangerous. Recruits had been known to fall off hilltops that had been underestimated. But the worst part was the recruits themselves. Exhausted from a 5 a.m. start, the short fuses and aggression kicked in, testing our teamwork abilities.

I could see Sullivan out of the corner of my eye and wondered if we would be put in the same patrol. A part of me wanted to be because he was a good team player and a brilliant navigator. Unlike most of us, who relied on map-reading skills to pave our way, Sullivan would go by his senses and only bring out the map to check his bearings. He was a natural and the staff knew it; he just had to be careful not to get injured. Another part of me didn't want to be put in his patrol. It might be awkward between us. What if the other lads picked up a vibe and then started spreading rumours? What if it gets back to Briggs? That would be terrible, not only for me and Sullivan, but also for the colonel. The staff could use it as a reason not to have any more girls coming through. I recalled hearing something about the navy and how girls were not allowed on submarines because they were seen as a distraction. Was this the same for women on the frontline? Would a lad feel the need to look after a female buddy more than a male buddy?

'Sir,' Digsby piped up.

I looked around remembering where I was and realised I'd probably missed the main part of the briefing.

'What?' Briggs looked irritated by the interruption.

'What are the timings?'

Briggs let out a sigh and looked round at the rest of the recruits. 'Lads, can we leave the stupid questions till the end?' He turned back to the map. 'The timings will be given last, like in all briefings.'

I glanced round at Digsby, who was now sheepishly staring down at the map. My eyes slid across to Lewis, stood beside him, and couldn't help smiling as I noticed a perfect arch of mud across his back and right arm, remembering Sullivan's comment about slipping near the shithouse with his weapon.

'Wanna share the joke?'

I spun round to Briggs, who was looking straight at me, face deadpan.

My lips quivered but nothing came out.

'You'll be leading a patrol tonight,' he said pointing the blade of grass at me. 'That will sort your fat arse out.'

I wondered why he kept calling my bony bum that. Perhaps his wife had a fat arse and he didn't have the heart to tell her.

Ten minutes later I was stood with my patrol, made up of some lads from 'E' Squadron, the Welsh crowd.

My map-reading skills were not great at the best of times, let alone in the dark. Neither were my communication skills with this lot. God knows how they felt about me leading them out tonight but I couldn't let their hostility cloud my thinking. Nor could I afford to show any signs of weakness, no matter what happened. I raised my heels off the ground a few inches to give me more height next to them.

A small van appeared from nowhere.

'Get in,' a mean-looking staff ordered us.

We all piled into the back, the door slammed closed, leaving us in complete darkness, then drove off. I couldn't sense any of the others around or the terrain except that it was bumpy, hurting my bum on the cold metal flooring. It felt like we had been travelling an hour before the van stopped, then the doors opened to a dim light from the moon above. We grabbed our weapons and scurried out. I panicked as I couldn't see anything or anyone. I tried to adjust my eyes to the darkness and eventually shapes of the landscape began to appear as the lights of the van came on and then faded away as it drove off.

The lads looked at me, waiting for instructions. I pulled my laminated map out from beneath my smock and switched my pen torch on, feeling them stepping closer and towering over me. My eyes bounced around the contour lines on the map, then out onto the landscape. We were stood around trying to figure out where we were and I had no idea. I checked my bearings with the compass then led the patrol into the darkness of the Brecon Beacons. At intervals we would stop, I would go out, do a recce of the area, then come back and brief the patrol on our next manoeuvre. We stopped at a point where the map indicated a forest but seemed like it had recently been cut down. This must be it, I thought.

Just at that point, Staff James appeared from nowhere and stood behind us listening in. I'd seen him earlier, following Briggs around. He reminded me of one those National Front lads who'd chase me when I was a kid, but an older version.

I tried to change my tone to sound more authoritative but it came out like a bag of nerves, then I headed out to do another recce, leaving my patrol behind.

I trod through the open ground, gripping the metal of

my weapon tight. I wondered if Staff James was speaking to the rest of the patrol to see how I was leading, but he wouldn't do that, I argued back, wondering if he was following me instead. I must be going the right way otherwise he wouldn't be here.

I felt myself filling up with hope as I warmed up to this new role of leading a patrol. It made me more alert, I felt a sense of responsibility for my men and I was finally feeling like part of a team.

It must have been only 100 metres I walked before I suddenly felt like I was walking on air. Before I had time to figure out what was going on, my body suddenly plummeted down. I lost control of my arms and legs, a sudden rush of air hit my nostrils, then... splash! My whole body was immersed in cold water. The weight of my kit pulled me down deeper. I was sinking, couldn't breathe, couldn't think. I struggled with the straps of the Bergen but the weight pulled me deeper into the water. It was too late. I struggled a little while longer, then stopped. My mind closed down into a sleep.

A hand suddenly grabbed me roughly by the collar of my smock and pulled me up. The air hit my nostrils, water was stuck at the back of my throat making me choke and splutter loudly as I was dragged up a bank. My body felt too heavy to do anything but go with it. The water dripped off my crap hat and onto my face – somehow it had stayed on. All I could hear were lads' voices around me shouting orders at each other. Somehow I managed to roll to one side then stand up, remembering where I was and what I was doing. But then something worse than drowning happened; I looked down at my hands then back up to the lads who followed my gaze. They knew what I was thinking.

I'd dropped my weapon in the river.

I was devastated and embarrassed because we all had to get in the river and find it – there was no way we could go back without it.

Twenty minutes later, my patrol and I were soaked, but I got my weapon back. I was livid, about to break down, but tried not to show it. I had no idea where the staff was but he had witnessed it all. It was over. I was going to be sent back to London.

The lads stood around me, hands on hips, seething, dripping wet. I gathered my thoughts because I still had to lead the patrol back.

'OK, listen…' I began.

They were listening alright, I imagined; they probably want to take this laminated map I was holding and ram it down my throat.

I gave the orders as best I could without looking at them, then we went on with me in front. We skirted around the river I had fallen in and across the mountains.

It was getting late, we were all tired from the river drama and I was lost again, so we bashered up on a boggy marsh to get some kip. Nobody spoke to me but I was past caring; I just wanted to get back.

I tried to sleep but was too wet and cold so I walked around for a while until I could no longer stand up. My mind hit a wall, my body crumbled into a heap under a pine tree, my eyes closed and I was running through that forest again with the pack of wolves.

An hour later I woke up to three faces I didn't want to see – the lads that pulled me out of the river. We got our kit together and began tabbing. Finally we reached the area, just before reveille.

Staff James was already back, waiting. He still had to debrief us.

''Ere they are,' he said, standing with the rest of the training staff, watching our weary faces as we put our Bergens down. Briggs was amongst them and it was the first time I saw him smile, revealing a massive gap between his front two teeth.

I prayed it would just be a screaming, I could take that. It's the other stuff I could do without, especially when we had an eight-mile run to do in less than an hour's time. My shoulders were killing me after carrying a stupid radio that one of the lads had put in my Bergen en route. I could smell breakfast being cooked in the staff truck.

Never in a million years could I imagine eating bacon or sausages, but the smell was making my mouth water.

I sat on top of my wet Bergen with my patrol, feeling miserable and shivering in my wet clothes as Staff James prattled on about the exercise, describing us as a bunch of losers.

I was only half listening. My mind wandered off to how I would be sent back to London. Would they do it tonight or first thing in the morning? Worse still, would they make me finish the weekend training before letting me go? The only other thing I could do was ask for my admin post back with Captain Wood, but that would be mortifying. How demoralising it would be to do paperwork for other girls coming through, while I sat there a failed candidate. Just the thought was making me well up.

'And you, Ahmed … what the fuck was that!?' Staff James's eyes bulged with anger.

I looked at him, not knowing what to do. Inside I was broken into a thousand pieces.

'You sounded like a drowning duck. You could have got your men killed with all that noise.'

My eyes prickled. I couldn't believe my efforts had been dwindled to the image of a drowning duck. Was this what the last year of hell had all been about? Whether they would discharge me or not, I was ready to throw the towel in.

We were eventually dismissed so we all headed to the the area where the recruits were getting bashered up. They were getting ready for the morning run. I scanned around for Becky. I didn't have time to put up my poncho and was going to ask Becky if I could share with her. Reluctantly I went behind a tree trunk, peeled off my wet clothes and changed into the dry kit which was in my wet Bergen. It turned out to be a useless exercise because, after the river, they were just as wet as the kit I was wearing.

I heard the recruits moving and went to join them, slinging the Bergen over my shoulders.

The run started up a muddy track congested with stones. There was lots of shouting by staff urging us to run faster. Sullivan ran up to me from behind. 'Alright, Ahmed?' he muttered under his breath. I guessed he had heard about last night's ordeal by now. How kind of him to ask, I thought. He risked that split second of slowing down to do this when normally he was the dragon at the front. I wanted to turn to him and say something but instead stayed focused on the run. With that he was off like a shot, weaving through the lads up to the front.

I was falling back a lot further than usual. I'd managed to take a couple of painkillers to ease the pain from my hip, which seemed to be working, but mentally I'd hit a wall. I wanted to slow down even more. Taylor turned up from nowhere and stayed behind me. He was pushing me along with his usual aggressive comments. I worried that he may have caught Sullivan running with me earlier. I wanted to turn round and tell him to shut up but instead I widened my stride to get away from him.

Staff James was up at the front. He suddenly turned around and shouted something at the lads running alongside him. I didn't catch what was said but three of them ran back down towards me.

'Come on, lads,' Taylor shouted as they approached us. They began running in line with me. 'You get nothing until the last man is in.'

I thought back to the assault course and realised what was happening. Two of them grabbed an arm each and dragged me along while the third became a wall behind, setting the pace. My legs were forced to run faster than they could manage and their grip on my arms was pinching the skin so hard I wanted to scream out. Instead I repeated my mantra in my head: *it's only pain … it's only pain.*

By the time we finished, my sugar levels had hit rock bottom. I grabbed a dessert ration pack and wolfed it down with a couple of biscuits, watching the others light up the hexi burners and cook breakfast. I couldn't think straight any more. I felt more like a casualty or someone who'd been tortured than a recruit on training.

Briggs suddenly came over, which was always scary, and told Becky and me to sort ourselves out as the colonel had arrived. By the look on his face I think it was a surprise to him too. The braids in my hair had come loose, causing strands to fall around my shoulders, which I'd scraped behind my ears; my uniform was muddy and wet but there wasn't much I could do about that, and my weapon was still in a bad state.

Becky was off like a shot, frantically getting her kit organised. I tidied my hair as best I could and straightened the collars of my smock. It was all I could manage after the beasting this morning. It felt strange the colonel coming here, almost out of place. What did he want? My mind rushed with scenarios; perhaps he was going to tell us what was next on training, or maybe he had come to check we were being treated fairly. Worst case he was here to tell me I was off the course.

To my surprise it was none of these. The colonel took Becky and I to a bank side and sat down with his legs stretched out and head propped up on one elbow. He looked at our exhausted faces, paused for a few seconds, then started telling us a story of the time he did selection, describing himself as tired and wet like us. Some of the men were taking off their wet kit and changing into dry as soon as they got back after an exercise, but he didn't. The story went on for a while longer. I wondered where all this was going and tried to stay focused in case he asked us questions afterwards. But instead, he got up and left. I racked my brains, trying to figure out what the motto of the story was, but nothing came to mind. Perhaps he saw my wet kit and thought I'd done the same, not realising this was the dry kit I was wearing.

We joined the rest of the lads to get ready for the next exercise. I wondered what they were thinking; would they ask us what the colonel wanted?

I saw the Welsh crowd talking amongst themselves as I headed to my basha patch. They looked up at me as I walked past. My heart slumped as I thought back to the river fall and how I'd let them down. I decided to say something and apologise perhaps. But just as I stopped and turned round I caught one of them smirking at me.

They were mocking me.

These lads would love to have seen me cry and I wasn't going to allow that to happen. I didn't care any more … about anything … about being a woman … about having to prove myself. Why? I recalled an incident a few weeks back when we were picking up our weapons from the armoury and I'd overheard a couple of recruits talking about me being a tick in the box. I was so angry I wanted to stand on top of an ammo box and hit them both over the head with my pistol. How dare they? I was going through the same shit as them, carrying the same weight; I was half the size they were, covering the same ground and not once had I moaned. Why couldn't

I be accepted as one of them? So what if I'm a different size, gender, race and religion? My mind was on fire.

I marched into the woods and headed to a patch where the lads normally pee and had one myself; arse in the air, breaking wind as loud as I could.

I will shit where you shit! I wanted to scream, but instead pulled my pants up and purposely walked past some lads with their backs to me having a pee. I sensed their discomfort as their voices trailed off when they saw me. It felt good.

I walked back to the basha area to change back to my other wet kit that I'd hung out to dry. This time I didn't hide away under my basha or behind a tree but stood outside in full view and got changed.

The lads nearby stopped what they were doing and stared.

'What?' I snapped back.

Lewis was the only one who reacted, while the others remained dumbstruck. 'Nothing, Ahmed,' he laughed slowly shaking his head. 'Nothing.'

Sullivan appeared on the scene and stood in my line of vision, trying to get up to speed with the situation. He still had my cleaning kit. I'd tried to avoid him since the run this morning and think he sensed it. My life was complicated enough and I didn't want to drag him into the chaos. He didn't deserve it.

CHAPTER TEN

LEARNING THE ROPES

I DIDN'T GET thrown off the course when we got back to London though I got a few surprised looks from the recruits when I turned up for the final phase of training, continuation. The numbers had now spiralled down to around forty men and two women: me and Becky.

Before it began, we got the terrible news that the colonel was retiring from the army. The leaving ceremony was heart-wrenching. All the soldiers and trainers were present in the big hall at the Chelsea Barracks. The usual buzz from the soldiers was now a low hum, which faded into silence as the colonel entered. He was escorted in by the adjutant; a beefy chap with hulk-like biceps bursting at the seams. The colonel stood on the stage behind the lectern, his tall body towering, and calmly looked over his audience. It felt strange to hear the leaving speech, especially as Becky and I hadn't finished our training yet. We only had a few weeks to go, and it was a shame he wouldn't be here to see us to the end.

I wondered what the new colonel would be like. I knew he wouldn't be as special as mine. My colonel had put his career on the line to put girls through selection training. He fought through the trainers' animosity towards us, kept an eye out for us. I wouldn't be stood here today if it wasn't for him. I was one amongst just a handful of women who had had the privilege of training with these men.

I noticed my colonel choking back tears as he came to the end. Tears sprang to my eyes at the reality I would never see him again. The applause was deafening as he walked off stage to be replaced by the new colonel. He was different. He didn't have the same presence as mine, or the strong aura and striking features. He looked about half the height, with squirrel features. His voice was not as strong, nor could I make head nor tail of what he was saying with all the acronyms flying around. The room was full of sad faces, still stewing over the now retired colonel. I wondered where he would be going. Rumour had it he was off to Whitehall, but nobody really knew anything except that we would never see him again.

I realised the impact that he'd had on me. The confidence to keep going stemmed from my colonel and now he was no longer here. Was I doing this for myself or for him? Both. We both wanted change. I wanted it for my life and he wanted it for the regiment. His absence left a big hole.

I wanted to ask Becky if she felt the same way but it didn't feel right. My relationship with Becky was still distant. She was a natural on the hills, which didn't surprise me considering she went rock climbing with the lads from the Para regiment. Recently I'd learnt she had also been the world champion in this sport.

For some reason I thought continuation would be easier than selection, mainly because I'd heard one of the trainers telling the lads that it was the best part of training. It was certainly different to the repetition we got on the hills. Continuation was focused on developing our skills in weapons, combat and covert. The one thing not mentioned was the sleep deprivation. I thought the hills were bad, but this was a killer. It was hard not to close my eyes, but once I did, it was deep, especially in lectures and demonstrations that required a lot of concentration.

We still worked in the field and were given a new set of trainers, which meant we got rid of Briggs, thank God. Not that these new trainers were any kinder. A few weeks into continuation, the number of recruits dwindled down to twenty lads, as well as me and Becky.

One evening, when we were sorting some food out before our next exercise, Becky came over with my cleaning kit.

'Thanks,' I said, putting it in the front pouch of my Bergen. I scanned the close vicinity for Sullivan. He was sat with some lads a few metres away. I felt terrible that I'd scared him off so much that he'd had to get Becky to give back my cleaning kit. Admittedly, I'd walked off a few times when he tried to approach me and ignored him when he tried talking to me – but I couldn't risk getting kicked off the course. Perhaps I was overreacting. Becky was talking to the lads all the time on the hills but no conclusions were drawn about her, so why did I think the situation was different with me? Maybe it was my deep-rooted culture still simmering beneath the surface, which I couldn't shake off.

My eyes came back to Becky, who was looking straight at me. I felt my face flush and had to turn away.

'Do we know what the exercise is tonight?' It was the first time I'd attempted to spark up a conversation with her.

'Same as always, we don't.' Her response was blunt and I could feel her still looking at me.

It was a strange feeling; it was as if she was my mum

and I'd been caught talking to a boy. I tried to fight it off, telling myself that all we'd done was share a beaker of water to heat our ration packs. Maybe she could see the guilt on my face or maybe someone had said something. I looked around again and noticed Digsby going to the next exercise. He was ten minutes early, as always, so that he could be acknowledged by the trainers. Sometimes it's not good to be noticed, especially here. Pity he never came first on the hills. The muscle men had long gone from the training, along with the big mouths – all except Digsby. I had no idea why he was still here, but then again, I had no idea why I was either.

To our surprise and sheer delight, the evening exercise turned out to be a demonstration and talk by a medic on 'attending to an injured buddy'. We sat in a semicircle in the middle of the woods as he demonstrated on a dummy how to put a drip into someone. It was dark and the only aid was a dimly lit torch.

I could tell from the rest of the recruits' faces they were thinking the same as me – they couldn't believe we had been let off so easily tonight. We'd had a day of arduous training and had just eaten, so being sat here not moving was making us feel mellow and relaxed. I leaned back on my Bergen and stretched my legs out. Becky was sat a distance away from me watching the medic curiously. I couldn't stand needles and had to look away, even though the medic was demonstrating on a dummy. There was something about veins that made me squeamish.

The medic finished, then brought out a pack of drips and told us to pair up. We all suddenly looked around in a panic. I jolted upright; I would rather tab another fifty miles than let any of these lads poke a needle into my arm. By the look on everyone's faces I'd say they were thinking the same. Nobody was coming forward to partner up with anyone. We just sat there. Then, for the first time, the lads looked at me and Becky, hoping to buddy up with us.

Perhaps they thought that, being girls, we would be gentle. The only thing I'd seen of these lads was aggression and I couldn't even contemplate buddying with Sullivan, who seemed the most capable of them all. Becky and I shot a glance at each other then she got up and made a beeline for me. She almost ran in case one of the lads caught her on the way.

The lighting we had was bad, which was purposely done. Luckily Becky was gentle and I hope she thought I was with her too. I rolled up my sleeve and presented my arm, then turned away watching the others. It was a funny sight to see the lads looking so scared. Tempers were up, too, more so than I'd seen during night navigation on the hills. I could hear the stress in their voices threatening each other: Do it properly mate! … Easy now! … It's there! Are you fuckin' blind?!

It was a tense exercise but if anything it brought Becky and I closer together. We began to partner up more and talk openly with each other. All this was rewarding, a step forward with Becky, but I still couldn't tell her about the double life I was leading with my family.

Sullivan was still on the radar. I thanked him for giving back my cleaning kit and he asked if I wanted to grab a bite to eat one afternoon when we were unloading the truck back at Chelsea Barracks after training. I was taken aback by his offer, not sure how to react, then nodded without thinking.

The Stockpot restaurant across the road was not quite the place I imagined we'd end up. It was one of the few places I hadn't ventured because a lot of people from the barracks went there and it definitely lived up to its reputation as a community of vibrant characters out of uniform.

'Looks really busy in here…' I stopped Sullivan at the bottom of the stairs, catching a few faces looking up, their eyes flitting between us. 'Why don't we try somewhere down the road?'

But Sullivan wasn't having it. He guided me to a table where people were just leaving.

We sat down across from each other. The waitress came over, cleared the table and handed each of us a laminated menu, then disappeared. I was hungry but more concerned that someone from the barracks would see us together. The room became noisy as more people arrived. My heart skipped a beat each time someone came down the stairs and walked past us.

I felt guilty because Becky had asked if I wanted to go for coffee but I'd said I was going home.

The waitress came back to take our order.

'What you having, Pixie?'

I looked across at Sullivan. Pixie? Was that my nickname amongst the recruits or just with him?

To my dismay, Sullivan ordered pork belly and so I had to sit across from him and watch him eat pig.

'Thanks for my cleaning kit … giving it back I mean.' It came out all wrong but I'm sure he got the general gist.

He looked down at his dirty fingernails. I noticed a smile creep up on his face, making dimples appear in his cheeks. 'I think you're fuckin' mad.'

Here we go. 'To be doing the training?'

'Why the fuck? What do your family think of all this?'

'What do yours think?'

'They don't know, but that's different.'

I cocked an eyebrow, enjoying the banter. I didn't

get my horns out for a fight, I just wanted to know what he thought.

He leaned across the table and held his gaze with mine. I'd never looked a man in the eye so intensely before, it felt strange.

'Don't get me wrong, I think you're brave.'

Brave? I wasn't sure about that word.

'But I would be concerned about your safety if you were … you know, put on the frontline.'

'A distraction?' I offered.

'Your safety.'

'More so than a bloke?'

'Yes.'

'A hindrance?' Monty's words came back to me.

'Yes … no.' He battled with his words, which didn't give me much confidence.

But it didn't matter. I suddenly saw a very caring side to him, more so than I'd seen in the field. Were all the lads like this or just him? I was so used to doing things on my own, fighting every battle single-handedly; leaving home, getting through college, running my business, buying property, travelling abroad. I'd never been surrounded by the support of family or partners. It became the norm to do everything on my own. But being there with Sullivan that day somehow didn't make me feel that way.

Things had finally settled with my family. The whole hajj palaver turned out in my favour when Auntie Pataani turned on the waterworks about being alone. It made my parents' feel guilty and they offered to take her with them. I tried to hide my relief when Mum called up to give me the news. For some reason she thought I'd be disappointed. She tried to compensate by saying 'God willing' they would take me with them next time.

In some ways I was glad to have them out of the way. My feelings towards Sullivan were getting stronger. My heart pounded every time I saw him. It ran deep and I was afraid he could sense this. He'd catch me sometimes looking at him and I'd quickly look away with an exaggerated turn of the head.

After training I'd always hope he'd ask me out to the Stockpot again. Sometimes he would and I'd find myself applying a touch of mascara and lip gloss. We'd sit downstairs in one of the coves. I'd do most of the talking, encouraged by his trail of questions about my family and my life in London. I'd try to turn the conversation around but he'd always find a way of flipping it back.

Most of the time he'd leave the barracks with the lads, at which point I'd look for Becky and we'd end up going for coffee and cake then head home. I began to learn a lot about Becky and discovered parallels in our lives. Her father was in the armed forces in South Africa. She left the country after apartheid and took up rock climbing; became an international champion then decided to join the British Army. Perhaps, subconsciously, we were both trying to take a son's role in our fathers' lives. The thought freaked me out.

My parents' trip to Mecca extended to Pakistan. They arrived back at the tail end of the continuation phase of the training. It felt like ages since I'd been to Manchester and when I did go, I found that things had changed. The war on terror had intensified; Blair's and Bush's claims were hitting the headlines fast and furious.

The debates flared in the living room, dominated by anger over the British intervention in the Middle East. Visitors stayed longer, which meant there were more cups of tea to be made. My mum would sit in the middle like a political adviser and talk about what people already knew … yes, the Twin Towers had been hit, yes, the government blamed bin Laden, and yes, America created the monster in the first place. The chatter was fascinating; Blair's conspiracy, Bush's cunning plan to get the oil. I gave the whole topic the benefit of the doubt. If there were weapons of mass destruction, which would endanger the lives of millions, then something needed to be done.

My political history wasn't great so whatever snippets

I captured from the news I tried to piece together. Although there was anger at Bush's response in attacking the Middle East, the community mourned the dead. Lives were lives at the end of the day, and the media wasn't helping by televising the terrorists and promoting Islam as a terrorist religion.

I didn't see Shazia during my visit and perhaps it was for the best. I'd heard she was now wearing a full burka.

Back in London, security was tight at the barracks. The lads in my unit wouldn't ask me directly what my views were on 9/11; some of the less educated would pull a face when I walked past, which was good because I knew not to waste any time with them. I'd seen this kind of behaviour happen in many communities throughout the years; a few individuals who spoilt it for the majority.

Sullivan's behaviour, however, surprised me more than anyone's: he became protective towards me. He'd go out of his way to be by my side; be it on exercise, in the classroom or on parade. Sometimes he'd even make a beeline for me, causing a stir amongst the recruits. But I think he purposely did this to send a message.

'Alright, Ahmed?' he'd say.

'Yes,' I'd reply. I can look after myself, I wanted to add, and remind him of the 'sticks and stones' rhyme.

He'd make a point of walking me out of the barracks, causing some of the soldiers to stop and stare. Sullivan would give them a hard stare back, at which point their faces would soften and then they would smile at me. I wanted to stick two fingers up at them but resisted.

As time went on and the government's reasons to invade Iraq weakened, my views began to waver. On the one hand it was what these lads had been waiting for – to put their training into action – but I couldn't agree that the war was fair. A lad once told me in the unit that the army's main roles were to prevent wars and stabilise conflict areas, which was heart-warming, but this intervention didn't feel like it fulfilled either of these roles.

It was at this point that I began to pay attention to the army's role in global conflicts, past and present. I turned on the news more to follow current events. I reflected back on the last invasion, after Kuwait was attacked, and began to understand Dad's obsession. Nobody else in the household took an interest. I wish I knew then what I know now and had taken the time out to watch the news with Dad and debate matters.

It was difficult to voice my opinions at the barracks. If I said I wasn't sure about the Iraq invasion I might have been accused of being a traitor, I thought. But if I said I fully supported it, I could imagine the surprised looks I'd have got. Would they react the same way if Becky opposed the war? I wondered. I shouldn't care what anyone thought of me, I told myself. I couldn't change the way other people thought, but I could change the way *I* did.

* * *

'Cagney! Lacey! Over here.'

Becky and I grabbed our weapons, like the TV cop girls, and scurried over to join the line of men sat on the classroom floor with their weapons in front of them. Tonight we were back at Chelsea Barracks doing our regular weapons class.

Staff Carter was one of our trainers on this phase. He was a tall, lanky chap with hawk-like eyes. His voice was far more controlled than the others, which made him scarier in my opinion.

He had it in for me from the moment we met, especially when I took his weapon by mistake and used it all weekend without realising. I still have flashbacks from the punishment I received from him.

'Anyone want to start off by telling me what this is?' Carter held the same model weapon in his hands, pointing it down to the floor and looking through the eye piece. 'Ahmed?'

I looked up at him, wide eyed, heart in throat.

'Thinking?' he intervened.

I stared down at my weapon, trying to remember back to my notes from last week's class.

'The gun...'

'It's a weapon, Ahmed.'

He turned round to the lads and started talking to them, then knelt down on the floor and took the weapon apart, overwhelming us with information about each piece. His eyes flickered in my direction a few times but no further questions were asked – thank God.

I saw Sullivan out of the corner of my eye. I didn't want to look at him. I'd overheard one of the lads talking to him on the phone earlier before class as he made his way in on the train from Sheffield.

'What's he doing in Sheffield?' I had asked, wondering if his parents lived there.

The lad looked round, surprised at my curiosity. 'He lives up there with his girlfriend and kid.'

Thankfully the lad then looked away to check his text messages and didn't see my face drop.

I felt cheated. Sullivan had flirted with me when he had a family at home, which upset me more. For some reason I had thought I was special and now I felt like an idiot for thinking it could be anything more than friendship.

We followed Staff Carter's instructions, pulling our M16 weapons apart and going through the pieces and then putting them back together. I watched Becky clicking the pieces in place, and copied, but couldn't keep up, especially the last bit with the two semi-cylinder shells which were difficult to click into place because the weapon was long. Frustrated, I stood the weapon on its butt, wrapped both hands around the cylinders and firmly slid my fingers up and down a few times.

'Take a grip of that, Ahmed!' Carter shouted.

The lads looked round at me and roared with laughter.

I didn't understand the joke and carried on clicking it back in place. I wasn't in the mood for childish pranks. We were a week away from finishing, and I was anxious. The numbers had now gone down to about fourteen men left on training.

Past memories and future anticipations became one big blur in my head. The strange world I'd stepped into seemed to have impacted on me more than I'd bargained, not knowing from one day to the next what I'd be doing, except that it would be tougher. But there was also a strong sense of belonging to something, like a family. I recalled the first time we were taken for a warm up on female selection and spewing my guts out behind a tree, wanting to quit. Weeks passed, girls fell by the wayside; some from injuries, others just not turning up. The irony of how it ended, with the physically strongest and weakest girls together, no one would have guessed, not even the trainers.

There was a lot of guessing amongst the lads about what would be next for Becky and me, but nobody knew. Whatever it was, it had all been worth it to get here.

A young officer suddenly entered the room. Carter didn't seem to mind. He walked over to me. I was taken by surprise when he quietly asked me to go with him. I looked up at Carter, who gave me the nod. I placed my weapon down and followed the young officer out.

I wondered why Becky wasn't joining me. Perhaps they were giving us some assessment results, I thought, but couldn't remember anything being mentioned. I made my way along the empty corridor, behind the officer. The only sound to be heard was our boots squeaking on the shiny floor. It reminded me of my first visit; quiet and deserted.

I was summoned into an office where another officer was sat behind his desk busy scribbling away. He looked like he was in his early forties, with short, dirty-blond hair, matchstick moustache and sleeves rolled up to reveal hairy arms. He glanced up at me then looked back down and carried on writing. A female officer was stood behind him, which was strange. She was also wearing khaki, was in her late thirties, tall and slightly overweight, with hazel eyes and full lips. Her dark hair was tucked beneath her beret. I didn't recognise the regiment she was from nor did I know why she was joining us.

Finally, the officer put his pen down, told me to stand 'at ease' and began talking. The next ten minutes were a blur of confusing words, a lot of military terms that made no sense to me. Perhaps I wasn't meant to understand. He finished and I was dismissed.

Outside, I stopped by the stairway trying to catch up with everything I'd just heard. Something about not being allowed to finish the training course and for me to hand my kit back in. I stupidly hadn't asked any questions and had just stood there like a lemon. But what was I supposed to do, challenge my superior? It wasn't that Becky and I had been thrown off, I reminded myself – the whole programme had been cut, including the girls coming in behind us.

I suddenly felt angry. What was it all for? All those terrible panic attacks, the sleep deprivation, being ostracised, not to mention that my personal life had been turned upside down, my career was now non-existent and I was skint. Any chance of a relationship was now long gone, with or without my parents' blessing, as I had become a different person now.

I took a deep breath, tried to disregard the girl inside me screaming 'it's not fair' and headed back to the classroom in a zombie-like state. Carter looked over at Becky, signalling her turn. She looked across at me for clues, but I just picked up my weapon and began dismantling it.

Carter was part of this, I was sure. I wondered if any of the lads here knew, but guessed that if they didn't now, they soon would.

Fifteen minutes later Becky returned, looking devastated. The expression on her face was how I was feeling. Everyone couldn't help but stare at her.

'Are you OK?' Carter asked, as if he had to.

Becky shook her head slowly. 'No,' she replied. 'No, I'm not.'

I left the barracks after handing in my kit. It still hadn't sunk in. What was I meant to do next week: report to Captain Wood? I checked my phone and had a missed call from a number I didn't recognise, followed up with a voicemail. It was Liz, my friend from female selection. She was in the area at our usual place across the road.

Liz didn't look any different to the first evening we'd met; same hairstyle, same accessories, probably the same suit under that same coat. It did make me wonder if I looked any different. She began with the tradition of talking about the weather, then went on to the horrific train journey she had getting here, then to the latest headline on the news about the internet bubble burst and recession. I wasn't sure if she was saying this because she knew I was about to walk away from my company, but I didn't react. What surprised me most was that she didn't ask me anything about the training. Time ticked on and we got on to the second round of drinks and still not a word on the subject. Had she known that Becky and I would get thrown off? Why ignore me for months then call me up tonight of all nights if not?

'I was in Birmingham last week.' She took a sip of wine and looked me straight in the eye. It was a strange look, one I'd never seen before. 'Gorgeous Eid celebrations, did you get a chance to go home?'

I looked at her blankly as she carried on. I didn't know where this conversation was going but I didn't like it. She knew there was no way I could have gone home because of the training. I wasn't sure if she was doing all this on purpose, but it felt like a kick in the stomach.

Despite this, it was also pleasant to learn how culturally in touch she was. I wondered why I'd felt the need to hide this side of my life from the army? Just because I couldn't talk to my family about the army didn't mean I couldn't talk to the army about my family. It suddenly dawned on me that some of the lads probably knew more about Islam than I did from all the travelling they'd done around the world to Muslim countries.

'Liz,' I cut in.

She looked surprised by my interruption. I wasn't sure if it was because she wasn't used to being interrupted or just that it was coming from me.

'We got thrown off the course.'

I studied her face for traces of pretence but it all looked genuine. Her expression morphed from 'shock' to 'not surprised they'd do that' to 'anger'. The anger stage reminded me of Becky before I left tonight. For some reason she'd stayed behind to talk to the trainers about the decision and why the programme was cut. I wasn't sure how that would help; it's not civvy street where you can speak to someone superior to oppose a decision. The army had made their mind up and there was no going back.

'They can do what they want,' she finally said.

I couldn't argue with that and being a private I was more of a pawn in their eyes. I suddenly thought about the new colonel. Perhaps it was his decision to end it; perhaps he felt the regiment wasn't ready to have women coming home in body bags.

'Do you think they expected us to fail?' I tried.

A small smile escaped Liz's lips, more sympathetic than patronising, then she looked out of the window at the traffic on the King's Road.

'We can sit here and speculate all evening but we'll

never know the truth,' she said. 'But look at it this way, it would be worse if you got through then were given a desk job, especially as a private.'

I didn't know what she meant but knew she could see further ahead than me.

'So they had no intention of letting us get through?' I was going round in circles and she wasn't giving me a straight answer.

''Course not.'

Was this why she left, because she knew? Was this training just some political point-scoring game behind closed doors?

'You didn't think they would allow you both to walk through the barracks wearing a blue belt and sandy beret, did you?'

'Well, I…'

'You didn't think they would put women in patrols with these lads behind enemy lines?'

I opened my mouth to say something but she got in first again.

'You didn't think it was anything more than an experiment?'

I sat back for a moment and tried to soak it all up. How could I have been so stupid to have thought it anything more? I remember our colonel once saying that if the lads didn't take the women on training seriously, then it was a reflection of how the full-time 22 SAS soldiers felt about the TA lads doing the training.

And here I was, the bottom of the pile; a civvy trying to do something that people with years of military experience were trying to achieve.

'I don't know what I thought would happen,' I said. 'But this wasn't it.'

For the next few months I went on autopilot. Work was pulling me down; I clock-watched until 6 p.m. then went straight back to my empty flat. Very few things got under my skin, but this vacuum that the army had left was unforgivable, a betrayal at all levels. I thumbed through an old address book in an attempt to re-engage with friends I'd lost touch with since the training. Hardly any got back to me and I couldn't blame them.

I called home a few times, which surprised Mum.

'Is everything alright?' she asked.

'Yes, of course,' I lied. 'Just very busy…'

I could hear laughter in the background. Mum was entertaining again. I would never move back home but I suddenly had an urge for Mum's cooking, serving tea to guests, the noise, the chaos, my glitzy clothes. This had been my childhood, it was my family, my culture. It was me.

I decided to reach out to Nabila, an old acquaintance I'd met at a company launch years back. We connected straight away as her family were from Pakistan and Muslim, though she was Shi'ite and I Sunni.

She sounded pleased to hear from me and invited me to a Muslim women's event in east London. I was ecstatic. This was just what I needed: to build my own community, as Mum had done at home.

* * *

A strange, musty smell filled the air as I sat down and joined the girls in the small, dingy room, situated above a parade of shops in Bethnal Green. They were a mixed bag; Bollywood hair, boy haircuts and hijabs. I couldn't figure out what united them, apart from religion, of course.

There were eleven of us; three committee members sat at the back, enveloped in headscarves. We took turns to go to the front and talk about our adventures.

The most interesting topic was about life as a lesbian in Pakistan. The girl who spoke about it wore heavy, black-rimmed glasses, dungarees and Dr Martens boots. She paced the front while she talked, fists punching the air. I wondered how her boy haircut went down with her family. She told us of her time in Pakistan with her girlfriend and how they almost got caught in the act at her grandmother's house.

I felt a sense of belonging again. They were like a second family, like the one I'd had in the army. I was eager to get up there and tell my story. I envisaged surprise and respect for stepping into the army world, fascination about the double life I'd led with my family and pride about my patriotism for England.

But I was still bruised by my ordeal with the army. Liz was right: they break you down, mould you to their desire, chew you up and spit you out. I'd spent endless hours wondering where I would've been if I hadn't joined.

Nabila too had her story: married to a Hindu and becoming an outcast. She was a slight lady with spellbinding hips that swung like a pendulum. Her striking features comprised of almond-shaped eyes, thick eyebrows and shiny black hair pulled back in a tight ponytail. As always, she wore traditional clothing, regardless of the wintry weather; cotton shalwar kameez and flip-flops. She winked at me when it was my turn to go to the front.

I got a few encouraging smiles as I made my way to the front and gave my story about the army, portraying the positive aspects of my experience.

A hand went up.

Relieved by the interaction, I stopped to let her speak.

'Which army?' the girl asked.

I was confused by her question. Did she think I was in the Pakistani Army?

'This one…' I replied.

I waited for more hands to go up, glancing at Nabila, who began clapping. A few women followed suit which led me to finish and sit back down.

The evening ended with a trip to the local kebab shop, which was brightly lit with neon ceiling tubes. The men behind the counter wore tall paper hats, showing their teeth as we walked in. I could tell the place served good food because it was full of Asians. I was the first to order and took my shish kebab to a shiny plastic table that was nailed to the floor. I noticed the others taking their time at the counter and began eating slowly, wondering how I could get more involved. It felt like my teenage years all over again, trying to engage with the Pakistani girls in the community.

Nabila broke from the cluster and joined me.

'So when's the next meeting?' I asked as she sat across from me.

Nabila looked down at the kebab in her hands. 'Really sorry, Az … the committee leaders don't want you here again.'

I looked over my shoulder, noticed that the others had taken another table, and tried to push the hurt away.

'Why?'

'Because you were in the army and supported the Iraq War…'

I couldn't believe what I was hearing. I wanted to go over and strangle each one of them but instead turned my anger onto Nabila. 'Don't you think they are supporting the war by living here … paying tax to fund it?' I could hear my voice rising. 'Why introduce me to these morons?'

Nabila flushed red but I didn't care, I was hurting too. I stood up proudly and headed to the door without a backward glance, but deep down I was crushed. My friends had dwindled and I couldn't afford to lose any more, but it was too late.

The evening ended with a phone call from Becky with the terrible news that John Sullivan, who had recently left the army to work for a private security firm, had been killed out in Iraq. It felt like someone had punched me in the stomach. A memory floated to the surface: John sat across from me at a table in a greasy spoon having a mug of tea. It was the last time I had seen him. He talked about loving the outdoors, which I imagined his girlfriend probably hated. Though I sympathised with John, my heart went out to his girlfriend. These blokes live and breathe the outdoors, away from the central heating, as John put it, then they disappear for months on end abroad on army training. I take my hat off to every wife and partner of a soldier – I for one couldn't do it.

'When's the funeral?' I asked.

Becky gave me the details but said she couldn't attend so I got names of people travelling down from London to Godstone in Surrey, where the funeral would be held.

The next few days were a wipe out. My stomach churned every time I thought of John, which was quite often. How could he be dead? He must be out there somewhere, putting up a tent. A part of me was trying to find excuses not to go to the funeral as I wasn't looking forward to seeing those faces again from the barracks. I lay awake at night wanting to share the grief with someone but instead closed my eyes and did a special prayer for John.

On the day of the funeral I met a couple of lads at Paddington Station. We grabbed a table on a train heading to Godstone. The lads sat across from me yapping non-stop to each other about leaving the army to make more money. I wondered if John would still be alive if he hadn't left the army. It's tough enough for any soldier to adapt to the outside world, having been institutionalised for so many years in the military and not having to think about everyday civilian duties such as bills, travel expenses or food shopping. Add to that the contrast of entering a workplace that is not set up as robustly as the military's chain of command, management process and funding. The private security firms didn't have the same backing as the government; if a soldier got shot, the government came down hard on the enemy, but if an ex-soldier got shot, the private security firm had no clout. This was why the enemy would rather kill an ex-soldier than a soldier, given the choice. The figures of soldiers dying did not therefore reflect those ex-soldiers who were killed working privately on assignments on behalf of the government. The MOD had handed out the contracts thick and fast to these firms and new start-ups. As a result, it had led to rapid expansion, jeopardising management infrastructure to support the men who were active in foreign countries on dangerous territory.

The church in Godstone was packed. I wedged myself between two burly men, their wives on either side holding their hands for support.

I spotted John's mum coming in; a timid-looking lady. Her eyes were lifeless. Her cheeks hollow, skin red and lips cracked. What could anyone say to a woman who'd just lost her child? The confusion and anger she must be going through, I thought, especially knowing that her son was doing a dangerous job, must have been overwhelming.

They say the grieving cycle takes a month to get through, which is about the same as the forty days Muslims are given to formally mourn for the dead. After today, the rest of us would go back to our normal lives, but for John's parents the death of their son would leave a big hole in their hearts.

A few familiar faces dressed in dark suits and ties were amongst the crowd. My eyes skidded to Briggs. He still scared the hell out of me.

Then I looked over my shoulder and spotted my colonel sat at the back alone. I decided to go over afterwards to tell him what had happened with the training and how angry I was about it.

But then I suddenly realised how wrong I was. It would be easy for me to take this unwelcome news as a downward plunge and allow it to have a negative impact on my life, whereas as a result of all I had experienced and endured, I could successfully rebuild a new life. The army had taught me a lot; discipline, teamwork, connecting with people from all walks of life and, most importantly, I'd learnt a lot about myself.

I stared until I caught the colonel's eye. We exchanged a smile then I turned back as the service began. Tears streamed down my face. I sniffed loudly. It didn't matter because the sound of the organ drowned out the noise. Regret kicked in. I should have stayed with Becky after that weapons class, during which we got kicked out, and challenged the decision. I should have asked questions even if I might have been given no answers.

I wanted to know why the training was initiated in the first place, why it had stopped, and where we would be now if the training had continued.

My thoughts raised other poignant points. Would the bar be lowered for women on the frontline? How differently would feminist groups, who perceive the army as an old-fashioned, sexist establishment, react? Would British Muslim communities be curious to know how I was received in the army and why I did the training?

All positive initiatives, such as this had been, demonstrated a big leap forward by the British Army on religion, ethnicity, gender and international liaison. Moulds were broken and mindsets changed.

I stood on my tiptoes and spotted John's parents in the front row of the church. No parent expects their child to go before them. How do atheists cope with death? I wondered. Do they believe their loved ones just deteriorate in the soil, that there is no afterlife or chance of ever seeing them again?

A women holding a child around her waist joined them. I stared at the child, trying to find some resemblance to John. I couldn't imagine what it would be like to grow up without a father. I appreciated the stability that two parents provide and wondered if I would have turned out different if I'd been brought up by single parent.

The man beside me offered me a Kleenex mini-pack. I looked up into his puffy, red eyes and started crying again, uncontrollably, putting my head on his clean blazer arm and sniffling into it. He didn't mind. I didn't care.

The ceremony finished and I wanted to find my colonel. There was so much to ask. Gently I weaved through the people as everyone headed out to the burial. The colonel was a very tall man so he shouldn't be hard to spot, I thought. I stayed behind for one final scan, but with no success.

Gutted, I followed two lads out. They were discussing the family decision not to have a military funeral. John's father didn't want to have anything associated with the military as part of his son's funeral, though a few of the men had tried to persuade him otherwise. I could see where the father was coming from: this was about his son, not the military.

I stepped forward to join the queue of people shaping up to pay their final respects. The coffin was lowered into the ground. I shuffled forward, scanning the close vicinity for familiar faces.

A lad holding a sandy beret walked to the head of the coffin, bent down and bowed, then dropped the beret inside.

I looked away, hoping there wasn't a big drama. They

may oppose the father's wishes, I thought, but they had to respect them.

It was my turn. I walked over and knelt down, staring into the six-foot-deep hole. The beret had now slipped down the side of the coffin. The shape of the box made my stomach lurch. I couldn't believe John was lying inside about to be covered with dirt. I couldn't think of anything to say, stood up, blinked my tears and walk away.

Later we all crammed into a coach which took us to a community hall. I didn't recognise anyone on the top deck. It reminded me of the minibus that used to take us to the Brecon Beacons, except these guys were wearing suits. I wish I had left when the colonel did, as I couldn't see much conversation going on between me and this lot and I would probably end up standing on my own like a lemon.

The community hall was crowded and it felt like more people had joined. I walked through small clusters of people chatting amongst themselves, not sure where I was going. A few looked in my direction, then looked away.

No familiar faces, then suddenly I caught a woman's eye. It took a few seconds, then it came back. She was an officer, on female selection; one who'd left on week three.

She stood amongst a few men from our unit, chatting away. I became self-conscious and intimidated because she was with people and I was on my own.

I headed over and she smiled as I approached her side.

'Hello,' I said, relieved that she recognised me. I tried to sound casual but it came out serious and loud.

'Is Becky with you?' she asked.

Why did everyone think we were joined at the hip? I recalled Captain Wood nicknaming us 'Tweedle Dee' and 'Tweedle Dum'.

'I'm trying to find John's parents.'

'Over there somewhere.' She pointed across the hall at a partition wall where a small crowd were walking slowly around, looking at photographs that had been pinned up.

I didn't want to see any photos of John – too painful.

'So what are you and Becky up to now?'

I didn't know what to say. I had no idea what Becky was doing, though I had heard through the grapevine that she was becoming a successful motivational speaker, rubbing shoulders with television producers.

I felt like a failure; to have not seen something through to the end was something my father would never allow.

The woman was still looking at me, sipping her wine, lips curled up. I felt embarrassed. I wanted to leave, but first I had to find John's parents.

'Excuse me.' I pushed through the crowds as politely

as possible, making a beeline for the photo wall. A few familiar faces watched me with poker faces. I'd ignored them.

As I approached the photo wall, I found it hard to stop the flow of tears as John smiled back at me. Memories of the training came flooding back, all the good ones of John and I sharing moments together. I wished I'd spent more time with him and regretted the times I'd ignored his requests to engage.

What was it all for?

'Good little Muslim girls shouldn't be drinking.'

I spun round to see Briggs, who was supping a pint, then felt my fingers tightly clench the glass in my hand.

I nodded, not knowing what else to do, and took a gulp of ginger ale. It went down the wrong way and I tried to choke inwards, hoping he wouldn't notice, before turning away and spluttering uncontrollably.

'Well, Ahmed,' Briggs continued, oblivious to my sounds. 'You got treated the same as everyone else … no special treatment…'

I wasn't sure what triggered this, but I wanted to stop him and say that I never expected to be treated any differently to the lads, which is why I respected him and the other trainers. What perception did they have of me? That I was a winger?

A few lads barged into our one-way conversation.

Briggs became engrossed with them, laughing and revealing the big gap in his teeth.

Twenty minutes later I was stood in the rain on the empty platform at Godstone, staring down at the tracks. How surreal to see the trainers and my colonel again. It was hard to believe I once belonged to this world. I wondered where I would be if I'd got a brown envelope through the post, calling me up for service. Would I have done it? If it meant helping to stabilise countries of conflict, I would be proud to be part of it, but I couldn't help wondering if this war was worth dying for? How long will it go on and will it prevent a bigger war from happening in the future?

Was this what John was thinking when he went out there? I wondered. He was a good man, always looked for the best in everyone and would always go out of his way to support the weakest. I now realise how big an impact he had on me during the training; always asking me how I was getting along, encouraging me every step of the way. He was the only one I could share my tears of pain with. I have a lot to thank him for and regret not telling him this when he was alive.

CHAPTER ELEVEN

A LIFE IN PROGRESS

O N THE UPSIDE, my toenails have regrown, my blisters have gone and I can shave my legs.

The training was an opportunity of a lifetime. I have become a different person, my whole outlook on life is different. Perhaps if I hadn't done the training I might still have been engrossed in the corporate rat race, with more money but not the priceless life experience the army has given me.

It should come as no surprise that my parents were still on my back about marriage. They began to show signs of desperation by saying that I could choose my own husband as long as he was Pakistani, spoke Punjabi and was from the same caste. After months of radio silence they came up with another suggestion; I could choose my own husband as long he was Pakistani and from the same caste. Later, this dwindled down to marrying anyone as long as he was from the same caste, down to 'Just marry someone!'

So far, I haven't.

Perhaps they thought I was a lesbian?

My reaction was to defend myself or just plain ignore them. But as time went on, things began to shift around me. My friends settled into relationships – real relationships, similar to the ones my siblings had. Those who remained single, like me, felt they were missing something and became active in finding that special person to share their life with.

I couldn't understand why I didn't feel the same way and found myself on a journey of self-doubt, confusion and even forcing myself to match these feelings. Perhaps my father was right that I was too self-sufficient, perhaps I didn't carry that particular chromosome, or perhaps having witnessed the attitudes of recruits towards relationships I was scared. For some men at the barracks it was a way of life to have a few women on the side while married and it was accepted as part of the squaddie culture. So what was the difference between them and the Muslim men who had three wives and treated women as second-class citizens? The values I had run away from were here again, but just in a different environment.

I do wonder what my parents' reaction would have been if they had discovered that I was once in the army. The best scenario with Mum would have been for her to realise I was just a reflection of herself; fighting for recognition as something other than a subservient figure in the family. Her need to get me married was to prove she was capable of also carrying out the family duties.

As for my dad, perhaps he would have been proud of my military life, causing a special bond to be formed between us. Perhaps a part of me wanted to do the training to prove to Dad that I was just as capable as his sons, and that I could step into a man's world and do just as well. His army life was one he never shared with anyone; a life I wanted to be a part of.

I'm saddened my parents are not here today to read my book. They never did find out about my life in the army. Perhaps Dad would have been proud that I had entered his world after all.

Outside my home life, my relationship with Becky grew stronger once we left the army. We'd been through a unique experience together and the loss of it had left a big hole in our lives on a physical, mental and emotional level.

Becky went on to pursue a career as a climber and

became a successful motivational speaker. Some of the other recruits went on to join the regulars in Hereford, others left the army and joined private security firms, and a few decided to get out altogether and headed for a career in the City. Silently, I watched from the sidelines, feeling a deep void forming inside, wondering where to go.

My interest in the military continued. I started a civilian job with the MOD by chance, working on campaigns to recruit soldiers for Afghanistan. It felt good to be back on old territory; working with retired colonels, officers and majors who were brought in to assist on marketing strategies. It was then that I realised there were other ways to pursue my interest in the armed forces other than on the ground – by pursuing a political interest.

Politics had never been on my radar, though I had been influenced by my mother's salute to Margaret Thatcher on which party to support.

My hopes now were to give something back to my country and contribute to help make Britain a healthy society. I wanted to gain a better understanding of how our political conflicts around the world originated. Pakistan, a country close to my heart, puzzled me – why it had always remained corrupt and unstable compared to India, which it was a part of for many years. How a country whose name was invented by Cambridge professors – in fact an acronym comprised of the homelands that Britain owned – has now become Britain's biggest continuous threat.

I began reading the national news, then decided to dip my toe into the world of politics. Many doors closed on me, including my local council, which I had called numerous times and never received a response. How does one get into politics from the cold with no contacts in this world? I wondered.

By fluke, I came across a talk occurring at the House of Commons about women on the front line. Anything related to the army still interested me, so I decided to go, though later I realised the talk included journalists and aid workers working in areas of conflict. There was one high-ranking lady from the army who attended.

It took ages to get through security, then finally I arrived in the small, packed room. The panel was made up of several women and the three organisers were stood to the side. The army lady began to talk about her experiences of being a high-ranking female in the army, and what she saw as the future role of women in the field. Something made me put my hand up with a few others during Q&A afterwards and I asked her if she had ever heard of women 'perhaps' training with the SAS to also determine if there was a role for them in that unit.

'Never,' she said. 'I've never heard anything like that before and don't think it will be on the army's agenda.'

I sat back in my seat. If someone as senior as her had not heard about it then it had definitely gone into a black hole.

Afterwards I approached the three organisers, who were surrounded by ladies all wanting to ask questions. They were from the Conservative Women's Organisation (CWO). I managed to get the attention of one of them, Carol, who invited me to one of their workshops.

I rocked up in jeans and trainers and thought I was in the wrong place when I saw the ladies dressed in suits and pearl necklaces … God knows what they made of me. Thankfully, Carol welcomed me with a warm smile. The workshop kicked off with a branding exercise where we were put into pairs and asked to write first impressions of each other. My partner put me down as 'friendly but reserved', 'streetwise' (probably because of my dress sense), and 'from somewhere in the north'.

We moved on to selection questions, where each of us had to stand in front of the group and answer questions based on current affairs, with a few personal questions thrown in the mix. When it came to my turn, I froze at the first two questions; firstly because I've never done any public speaking, and secondly they were asking *my opinion*. Nobody had asked for my opinion on anything before.

'Ah, this is a popular one…' Carol wrapped up with a final question for me. 'Is there anything about your past which would embarrass or jeopardise the party or yourself?'

I asked her to repeat the question to give me more time. Paranoia kicked in, was it important to tell her about my army training, and that I hadn't completed the course for reasons unbeknownst to me?

Carol waited a few moments and then interrupted my thoughts. 'Think front cover of the *Mail on Sunday*...'

It took two years and a very steep learning curve to get through the applications, interviews, assessments, campaigning initiatives and political knowledge pool to finally be selected to stand as a parliamentary candidate in the 2015 elections.

People kept telling me I'd got into politics at the right time, when parties were looking for people with a variety of backgrounds and experience, rather than just career politicians. It was good to hear, but, at the same time, I didn't just want to be a tick in the right box.

My first stab was at becoming a councillor. I called up my local council and nobody bothered to get back to me, until Carol got in touch, at which point they returned my call. It was very hard to come in from the cold with no background in politics. The council I became involved with was friendly but distant, a different bunch. It wasn't a support group like CWO – we were all out for ourselves to get councillor positions.

The experience was not brilliant. Most people had an extremely high opinion of themselves, which I didn't like at all. And, for all that self-importance, when I got to the bottom of some of them, their day job was nothing to write home about… I'd done so much more with my life, but perhaps with my northern accent, ethnicity and gender, they didn't feel the need to ask about me and had maybe already made up their minds. I couldn't be sure this was the case, but I could sense it was.

Not surprisingly, I was put in a ward where I wouldn't have a chance, but perhaps all this was for a reason. As soon as I realised that I didn't have a cat in hell's chance of winning, I moved onto plan B: I would go for the elections the following year.

First, however, I had to pass the Parliamentary Assessment Board (PAB). I went into it a little late but was still determined to go for it. It would be an amazing experience to pass my PAB and run for a parliamentary seat. Both the Conservative Women's Organisation and Conservative Campaign Headquarters (CCHQ) were very supportive and steered my application in the right direction, and within weeks my assessment was arranged in Cambridge.

Before I left, Carol gave me two pieces of advice for the assessment: have an opinion on anything they ask, and be yourself. And that was exactly what I did. I had no idea about some of the questions asked, but I still said something. I also mentioned running my own business, my army experience, working for a homeless charity and being a governor at a special needs' school. This, if nothing else, set me apart from the others – lawyers, lawyers and more lawyers. Perhaps this is what got me through, as my political knowledge was definitely inferior to theirs.

I was thrilled when I got a letter to say I had passed. Next came the application, which needed to be well thought through. I lost count of the number of drafts I put forward to Carol to look at until I got the template right. To my surprise, I received quite a few invitations for interviews, from Sunderland to Wales, but the ones that drew me in were from Manchester and its surrounding towns.

*   *   *

As the train pulled into Manchester Piccadilly, it was raining as always. I headed out before the crowds and made a beeline for the exit. I was very grateful to have been invited to the initial interview for the Oldham and Rochdale seats. They were unsafe seats, but that didn't matter to me – I wanted to go for it and experience what it was like to be on this journey. I had no idea what to expect.

As I walked through Manchester town centre towards

the tramlink, I looked across to Piccadilly Gardens and noted how much the place had developed. I reflected back on when I first left there for London many years ago and how much the place had come on since then.

The tram went through Oldham, then finally Rochdale, which felt like a different world – only half an hour earlier I was on the dazzling stage of Manchester, now I was definitely backstage. I could smell the poverty – the young mums pushing prams, teenagers hanging around with nothing to do. The roads didn't look clean, shops were either boarded up or had grills over their windows even though they were open. I almost stood on a used condom as I came out of the tram station.

It was like being in a time warp. The media coverage surrounding Rochdale since the last elections had not been good. Sex abuse and sex grooming – in the place where I'd grown up. My feelings were very mixed. The last time I was here was just before my father died and it had been too painful to come back since. However, the familiarity of the Rochdale and Oldham seats drew me to applying here. I didn't think I would get as far as an interview, but here I was.

Going through Oldham on the tram didn't feel right; I was so used to the big orange bus chugging away. Oldham town centre was busy, there were new shops and even a Muslim college. It felt like the English and

Muslim communities were more integrated here than when I was growing up, even with all the media coverage of terrorism in the last ten years.

Times had changed for the better, I thought. I recalled the dreadful Oldham race riots back in 2001. Though I was living in London and was in the army at the time, I would visit Oldham and encounter an unpleasant sting in the air.

The Rochdale Premier Inn, where I was staying for the duration of my trip, turned out to be miles away from the tram station, but it gave me a chance to see the place. I finally arrived and, within an hour, I was in a local taxi taking me to Rochdale Conservative Club.

Twenty minutes later and eight quid shorter, I arrived. It was pouring with rain. I hadn't thought my wardrobe through and, for some stupid, stupid, stupid reason, I had decided to wear a dress with flesh-coloured tights and heels.

The first step I took outside was into a big puddle, which resulted in murky water splashing all up one leg. The committee had decided to have the meeting in the pub below the Conservative Club, as the hall had been booked for another event apparently far more important than selecting a candidate for Rochdale.

The panel was sat on one table – all white, English people – with their wines and beers. On another table sat the candidates – all Pakistani men, bar one who was English. I could feel their disapproving eyes on me as they looked me up and down, no doubt noting my ensemble of dress and (now partially dirty) tights. I felt as if I had gone back twenty years; it was as if I were doing something shameful. I managed to raise a smile and joined the candidates.

'What's your name?' one asked, who introduced himself as Khalil.

'Azi,' I replied.

'Azi what?'

Here we go…

'Azi Ahmed.'

I knew why they were asking – to check if I had a Muslim surname. They all looked down at my legs again. Even the English man looked puzzled. I pretended not to care but deep down I did. How could I be so stupid?! After all I had been through and with everything I knew about this area, I thought, why the hell did I wear a skirt? Thankfully, the meeting commenced shortly after and we began talking about the process of selection. I felt like cattle on a catwalk. A couple of elderly ladies in the blue-rinse brigade, who were sat at the committee table, shouted out in chorus, 'S'cuse me!'

Khalil tapped me on the shoulder – they were speaking to me.

'What's your name?' the ladies asked.

'Azi ... Azi Ahmed.'

Khalil looked at me and said with a wink, 'You're in.'

We all had to decide which constituency we would go for if we had a choice, though it would be the votes that would dictate overall.

Of the three constituencies for which candidates were being chosen – Oldham, Rochdale and Heywood & Middleton – I wanted Rochdale the most. One of the Pakistani men put his hand up for Rochdale too, but the others, it seemed, were steering away from that constituency. The meeting ended an hour later and we were given the date of the selection interview, which would be after Christmas. I wondered why candidates for these seats were being selected so late in the day, and could only put it down to the fact that they were unsafe.

The next day I headed back to London feeling even more determined to get the nomination. I checked my email and noted a few more invitations to other constituencies, but my heart was set on Rochdale. It was therefore with great joy that, soon after the visit, I received an invitation to go back for final selection.

Over Christmas and New Year I read up as much as I could on Rochdale, as well as on its Labour MP, Simon Danczuk. He had written a book on Cyril Smith that lifted the lid on historic sexual abuse of young boys and, although it was by no means an enjoyable read, it provided a real insight into the power this MP had had over the local people, as well as how much the public's perception of politicians had changed over the years. They were seen as such powerful entities in those days – almost like royalty. Though my mother was a Thatcherite, she thought Cyril was an amazing man with great presence, and even my dad would stop and watch the television whenever he was on.

My research on Rochdale was eye opening: one in four children were living in poverty; school results were below average in Britain; and, on top of all that, there were the sex-grooming and paedophile scandals.

All too quickly, the day of the interview arrived. We had been told to prepare a five-minute speech on why we would make a good candidate, a question I had gone through several times before. I would deliver the speech, then there would be ten minutes of questions from the committee, followed by ten minutes of questions from the floor. I'd been on the BBC news website for the duration of my journey here and had read all the newspapers I could get my hands on, so I thought I was prepared for anything.

This time we had the hall above the pub for the meeting, which made me wonder how many people were attending, but before it began everyone congregated in the pub like last time. After a while, people started to make their way upstairs to the hall – all except the candidates, who had to remain downstairs. A few minutes later, Michael, the chairman, returned with a handful of small, folded pieces of white paper, each with a number on them that would decide the order of presentations. Sod's law, I got number one, much to the relief of the rest of them. They sat back at the table, sipping their drinks as Michael took me upstairs.

This time I had smartly thought through my wardrobe choice and had decided to wear formal trousers and a long-sleeved striped shirt, which was buttoned up to the neck. I followed Michael into the hall. I could only see the first few rows of people because of the lighting, but the silhouettes against the back wall made me convinced that the room was packed. I wasn't sure whether to remain standing or to sit on the chair behind me, but I decided on the former, considering my height.

As I walked onto the stage, someone wolf-whistled. I stopped, not sure if I had heard correctly, and looked over at Michael, who was looking into the crowd trying to figure out who it was. He was visibly shocked.

My voice was shaking as I did my speech. It didn't come out the way I had practised it in front of the bathroom mirror, but I bumbled through. To my relief, I got an applause at the end, which helped stop my voice from quivering. Then came the questions from the committee, the subjects of which ranged from Syria to pollution to the price of a pint of milk. I can't remember the last time I bought a pint of milk, given that these days the 2-litre cartons are more common, so I gave the price of that and saw a few cocked eyebrows. 'Where do you shop then?' someone shouted.

Thankfully Michael came to the rescue and opened the questions up to the floor. The first was whether I thought we were doing enough about Muslim radicalisation. Of course not, I responded, but let's start working with the families and owners of social media sites, rather than always pointing the finger at authorities, though they too have a responsibility.

They asked me about sex grooming, which I was expecting. 'Of course we have a problem with a selected part of the Pakistani community which needs to be looked into,' I offered. Finally, someone asked me my view about windmills in Rochdale. My mind went blank. Do they have them already or are they about to? I decided to do the most stupid thing on the planet and pretend I knew what he was talking about: 'If we get them in, it will be a great idea to help reduce pollution.'

'We already have them and we hate them!' someone shouted.

I could feel my face burning but carried on until my

ten minutes were over, then left the stage with a small applause following me off.

'That was rubbish,' I thought as I was escorted back downstairs. The one non-Muslim candidate, Ian, went upstairs next as he'd picked number two. The rest of them hovered around me downstairs asking what the questions were. To be honest, I told them, it all happened so quickly that I couldn't remember most of the questions, but the one about the price of a pint of milk stuck in my mind, at which point everyone went onto the Tesco website on their phones to check out the price.

After Ian, it was Khalil's turn, and as he went upstairs I asked Ian if he'd got the pint of milk question.

'I did and I gave them the price of 2 litres – my wife's just been on the phone having a go at me.'

When Khalil came down he had a big smile on his face. I guessed he had made them all laugh.

Once all the candidates had done their presentation, we all sat down and waited for the votes to be counted upstairs. I took my diary out of my bag and started to look at the dates for the other interviews, feeling low. Finally, we were summoned upstairs and asked to stand on the stage in a line. I watched as Khalil lost out on Oldham East. I thought he looked a bit miffed, but he was offered his last-choice constituency, which he accepted graciously. Last up was Rochdale – 'last but not least' – and then I heard my name being called out, followed by an applause. Stunned and confused, I looked around, not quite believing what I heard.

*   *   *

For some reason I wasn't looking forward to my next visit to Rochdale, which was due to take place in March 2015. It was my first visit since being elected and, although I'd had a lot of correspondence with my agent, Ashley Dearnley, I hadn't worked with him as yet.

I wore jeans and trainers as I was expecting to spend a lot of time outside. Unfortunately, I was a little late, which didn't go down well with Ashley judging by his silent response when I apologised. I got in the car and we went to our first rendezvous point, where we would be picking up litter. It was bitterly cold at that time in the morning, and even though I was wearing two pairs of gloves, by the time we met up with Gary, the volunteer who ran the event, I was freezing.

'I bet it's a bit colder here than in the south,' Gary offered sympathetically.

I started to nod, then stopped myself, suddenly remembering where I was and *what* I was in this town.

'Not much colder,' replied the parliamentary

candidate for Rochdale in a strong voice. I didn't want to risk anyone saying I couldn't take the weather, let alone represent the town.

After that, we went leafleting in another ward. I wanted to go inside somewhere to have a hot drink but it didn't feel right to ask. We cracked on, up and down the hilly streets, shoving the blue papers into every letterbox visible.

After a break, we were off to do some more leafleting, and then we shot off to a meeting with a candidate who had stood in 2010, Mohammed Salim. He was a nice chap, very approachable, and Ashley went out of his way to say that he was a good man.

We met Mohammed in Starbucks with his cousin Sameena. Sameena was a lovely lady who invited me to a Muslim women's event the next day. Great, I thought – in the diary.

'Have you got a headscarf?' she asked.

Why didn't I think of that?

'Yes.' I replied coolly. I'll get one from my friend, I thought.

At the end of the day I got on the train, feeling like an ice cube, and thought about the hot food and warm bed waiting for me at my friend's house. She'd offered me a place to stay while I was in Rochdale – so much better than going back to an empty hotel room.

I was shattered by the time I arrived, so I began to work out what time I would need to be up tomorrow in order to get to this Muslim women's get-together. It had been ages since I had been to something like that. I got terrible flashbacks that evening to when I was a kid and had to go to these sorts of events with my mum. I remember them being very intimidating, where a lot of women would look down their noses at each other, comparing daughter-in-laws and the amount of gold they had plastered on their arms. I'd hated it.

But now I was an adult, no longer being dragged there, but going of my own accord … kind of. Let's face it, I told myself, twenty years have passed and things will be different. I borrowed a black headscarf from my friend – black was safe.

Finally, I thought, I was going to grasp the woman's vote, which is what I needed to get ahead. Ashley picked me up in the morning and, as I rode with him to the venue, I realised how lucky I was to have him. He was a gentle man, softly spoken, and knew how to play his politics without shouting from the tree tops.

Ashley dropped me off at the event, and the chanting was loud as I joined the sea of colourful headscarves. I sat at the back and suddenly felt disappointed. These women were not how I expected them to be. Some British Muslim women are very forthright, but these all seemed very docile. It was another time warp; nothing had changed here for Muslim women in the past twenty years. My dreams were shattered – they won't vote for me, I thought, they'll vote for whoever their husbands ask them to vote for.

I left feeling low, especially about the women. My strategy was to retain the Tory vote and take the women's vote. I began to mull it all over as I waited for Ashley. I was just another woman to them, but if I had been Baroness Warsi, for example, the whole room would have stood up to attention.

I had a thought as Ashley pulled up. We were on route to do an interview with a local newspaper when I asked, 'What's it like here for putting posters up?'

I told him how the women's event had gone and said that I thought trying to get the Muslim women's vote was like flogging a dead horse. If I had a poster of me with Warsi in the shop windows of Asian communities, people would know who she was and maybe associate my campaign with her. Ashley liked the idea and suggested I email Warsi's office to see if she'd agree to it.

The newspaper interview went OK, though I was very nervous. Hopefully in time they would get better, I thought. I was back to leafleting that evening before the association meeting, this time in a marginal seat I had been asked to help out in, Bury North. Ashley came with me and introduced me to everyone.

'Who are you up against?' one of them asked. 'Is it Simon Danczuk?'

'Yes,' I replied enthusiastically.

'Oh … well, you've got no chance with him.'

'Thanks for the encouragement,' I replied flatly.

'Sorry, but it's true. You won't knock him off his perch, but good luck.'

Ashley and I went for a quick bite before the association meeting at 8 p.m. We went through the emails from local people on political issues as fast as possible and then I asked him about what the man had said about me not having a chance against Simon.

'It's a shame Danczuk won't meet you as he knows everything happening in Rochdale and has access to everything,' Ashley said. 'Shame he's not here today, he's in Westminster as it's Budget day.'

'He might meet me if I ask?' I prodded. 'I do want him to say nice things about me, if asked. I'm no threat to him, I live outside Rochdale and perhaps I could meet him in Westminster to discuss the issues in Rochdale.'

We headed to the association meeting, and arrived a little late. There were about twenty-five people there to discuss events running up to the elections. All the time my mind was running through the events of the past few days.

By the time I got back to London, my inbox was crammed with emails from more local campaigners. I resigned myself to the idea that this would be the case until the elections were over – and then they wouldn't be interested in my views.

One interesting email I received was from the producer of a television company based in Germany who said that they wanted to feature me in a televised documentary about how the parties were getting the Muslim vote. I thought this would be a great idea and perhaps the media exposure would mean that Warsi might want to join me. I jumped at the opportunity and Ashley agreed that it would be interesting, so I emailed CCHQ and Warsi's office about it.

That week, however, I also got the unfortunate news that in one of the main marginal seats in Dudley North, the Muslim candidate, Afzal Amin, had been accused of plotting with the EDL (English Defence League) and had been secretly filmed doing so.

However, in spite of all of this going on, I had to focus on myself and was mulling over what Ashley had said about meeting Simon Danczuk. I emailed Simon's office and arranged to meet for coffee the following week at Portcullis House in Westminster.

I sensed that at the beginning of our meeting, when I asked about the topical issues surrounding Rochdale

(Cyril Smith, the sex-grooming scandal) and how it had been as an MP tackling them over the past four years, Simon was a little guarded. We then started talking about the current elections, the introduction of the smaller parties – UKIP and various independents – and how they would affect the vote. I think he soon realised that I was no threat. This wasn't about politics per se, but purely a discussion about Rochdale and its people. One useful thing I did take away was that he didn't think that the Lib Dems, who were very close behind Labour in the last election, would do so well this time.

'How do you know?' I asked.

'I'm out every Sunday morning for four hours knocking on doors. Last election, every twenty doors I knocked on, more than half would say they would vote Lib Dem. This time round, I'm lucky if I get one out of the twenty saying they will.'

This was interesting news, as these votes would need to go somewhere and perhaps this was the strategy for us.

Simon also told me about another piece of news that had just hit the headlines that morning. He had been publicly criticised by the outspoken columnist Katie Hopkins for raising the Pakistani flag with the local community as part of a yearly tradition. Hopkins had come out and said that he was supporting the very men who had raped white girls. I later tweeted in support of the Labour MP and described Hopkins as 'culturally uneducated'.

Simon and I shook hands at the end and I thanked him for his time. He stood up and was about to leave, then stopped and said, 'By the way, I looked at your profile online. I think you'll make a good politician.'

I decided I liked Simon. Not only was he helpful, but he also went out of his way to spend time with me talking about Rochdale. How many MPs would do that with their opposition?

* * *

When I first went back to Rochdale, I thought it would be like it was when I was living in London as a student; instead it was completely different. I saw the town with a fresh pair of eyes, and I looked at the people in a different light. This was no longer the community that I had grown up in, where I was afraid of receiving a racist comment as I walked down the street or worried that someone was going to give me a dirty look for walking around on my own and report me to my mum. No, I was an adult this time, and this time I was coming here to help these people. I felt a sense of duty and protection towards them.

I had heard nothing back from Baroness Warsi's office, so decided to have some posters made up with just my photo on them, and I contacted a couple of my parents' old friends to see if they knew of any shop fronts that I could put the posters up in. I imagined cloth houses, butchers' shops and off-licences in Asian areas. Also, if I did it myself, it would be my opportunity to tell them what I could do for the people of Rochdale.

There were just six weeks to go before the elections when the news broke of a Rochdale family, with children, that was arrested on the borders of Turkey as they were making their way into conflict-stricken Syria. It turned out that a Labour councillor, Shakil Ahmed, was the father of one of the men being held at the border. The councillor said he thought his son was somewhere else, but I had a feeling that this would still cause a backlash against the Labour Party. However, Simon Danczuk rescued the situation by telling the press that the family that had run away would not be allowed back in Rochdale. He had a number of Muslim backers beside him when he made this announcement, and what pleased me was that the imams were finally speaking out in public, condemning ISIS and what they were doing to Muslim people. It has taken many years for this to happen. Also, the Muslim council had been on television many times to talk about the effect this organisation was having on innocent people and its brainwashing of young British Muslims.

*   *   *

Things were now cranking up. The emails from local Rochdalers were flooding in, especially now my leaflets had been delivered to over 30,000 Rochdale houses. Unfortunately, I got news from CCHQ that I was to cancel my interview with the German TV company. They didn't say why, but I thought it might be to do with the Afzal Amin scandal and 'how far will we go to get the Muslim vote?'. Ashley thought it would also highlight the sex-grooming issue in Rochdale.

Heading back to Rochdale once again, I decided to stay on the outskirts and see the countrified side of it. I was at a lovely B&B 2 miles out of the centre, on the hilltops overlooking the town. One of the main events on this visit was a hustings with the other candidates – seven in total. I'd never done anything like this before and I was nervous as hell. No matter how much I read the papers and watched Sky News, I didn't feel ready. The set-up for the event was for each candidate to give an opening statement, which would be followed by seven questions from the public.

I tried to cover as many topics as possible in

preparation – the EU, the NHS, environment issues, immigration, Rochdale facts and figures. I knew it would be Sod's law that they would ask me questions on the only topics I hadn't covered.

A few days before, I had received an email from an imam in Rochdale requesting a meeting. I arranged this for just before the hustings event and asked Ashley to come with me. 'It shouldn't take more than half an hour,' I told him. I had tried in the past to reach out to these religious leaders but couldn't get close to them – no doubt because I was a woman – and finally one had reached out to me. Even being able to speak to one imam was very useful. UKIP had selected an Asian man as its candidate and I was sure this was so that he could muscle in with the imams. Simon was already well connected with the religious leadership, which I thought had contributed to his last election victory for sure.

The imams were so important as they held the power in the Muslim community. I recalled what my father had said during the war on terror, when US intelligence services were working with the government. He said that power of the people is with the imams, not the government, and that politicians were barking up the wrong tree. Rochdale has a Muslim community that makes up around 13 per cent of the area's population, while the average in Britain is less than 5 per cent. I'm led to believe that the Muslim vote in Rochdale could make up around 6,000 votes. That's not too far off the total number that the Tories received in the 2010 general election.

Ashley and I arrived on time but the shop front looked closed, and all the shops around it either had metal shutters or boarded-up windows. I looked around at Ashley with a surprised look, but it apparently came as no surprise to him. He called the imam to find out where we should go specifically and we were directed to a backstreet car park. A bearded man wearing traditional shalwar kameez came out from one of the back entrances to greet us.

He took us upstairs, through a rabbit warren of tiny corridors and then finally to a room where we were greeted by eight men with beards and hats. The whole set-up was not what I was expecting. I thought we were going to have a quick chat over a cup of tea with this chap, but this looked like a very well-organised meeting. There was a table already set up with chairs for everyone and there were even snacks laid out.

It took me back to my mosque years and reminded me of the bearded visitors to the house who wore big hats, and, of course, my Bangladeshi imam. They may have reminded me of my childhood, but this was a completely different situation; no caning, no sinning, no ganging up with my parents to chastise me – we were now on the same level. I had hesitated earlier at the idea

of putting my headscarf on, and realised I was still pro-
grammed to cover my head when entering a room full
of men. But if I did this here, would I come across as a
subservient parliamentary candidate?

The meeting began with introductions. The man at
the head of the table introduced himself as the treas-
urer for Golden Mosque; the next along was the head
of the Rochdale council of mosques; then a few more
treasurers of different mosques in Rochdale. It suddenly
dawned on me that I had 6,000 votes sat in front of me.
Now it was my turn, and I gave them my usual spiel. I
was nervous and I could tell they sensed it.

I cut myself short just before I got to my army life – I
didn't feel it would help me here and, if anything, it might
have sent the whole conversation the wrong way. Then
the questions started coming… What were my views on
the Palestine/Israel conflict? If elected, how could I see
myself working with a Labour council? How would I
deal with the growing concern of Islamophobia and racism in Rochdale? Why is the government hunting down
Muslim schools and not Catholic ones? Why is Eric Pick-
les sending out letters to imams about extremism and not
to the vicars or priests? Why do we need to be earning
£18,000 to be able to bring someone over to this country
and not £12,000, which is the minimum wage? I tackled
the questions as best I could, but realised that, in all the

swotting I'd done that week, I'd hardly touched on the policies they were interested in hearing about.

These imams were well-read, extremely intelligent and, my God, they knew their politics. I think it would have been easier yomping my Bergen across the Brecon Beacons than being interrogated by these chaps. They were running circles around me.

They were interviewing all the candidates, they told me, as they wanted a change. They hadn't got what they were promised in the last election. That's when Ashley chipped in and said that the only alternative to Labour was to go with the Conservatives. I had to keep reminding myself that the last time the Tories even came close to winning this town was over fifty years ago, and so the only strategy I could hope to make work here was to ask the people to vote for the person, not the party. National politics will be what it is, but you have to choose the person you think will listen to you and who will make the necessary changes to your local area.

The imams expressed how racism had increased since the sex-grooming scandal and that they felt unsupported. The media was not helping, they said, and if they were going to vote for me, I'd better be media-savvy enough to represent them.

The meeting ended with a group photo, and, by the time we finally got away, we had been at the meeting for almost two hours. We had to hurry to avoid being late to the hustings. I'd only had a couple of slices of toast that morning, but I would have to wait until that evening for food.

My original plan was to arrive at the hustings a little early so I could mingle with the locals, and now I only had four minutes to do so. I had hardly got through the door when the UKIP candidate pounced on me, shaking my hand and introducing himself with a big smile. I moved on quickly and went to say hello to Simon Danczuk. I had to battle through his fan club to get to him, at which point I asked him how he was and how he was feeling about the event.

The top table had seven seats representing each of the party candidates: Conservative, Labour, Lib Dem, UKIP, Greens, an independent and a religious representative. I was the only woman.

Finally, we were told to take our seats. (I put two folded-up fleeces on mine and sat on top of them to ensure I was at eye level with the men.)

The event was hosted in a church, and, before we began, the vicar came and stood in front of us, facing the crowd. He invited everyone to 'join him in a prayer' and I closed my eyes and did so, remembering my mother's words that a church, just the same as a mosque, was also God's home. I thought about my parents and wished they were here today, sitting in the crowd and giving me support. Would they be proud that I had come back home to help the community? I wondered. After the prayer, the place felt peaceful and I felt relaxed.

The vicar opened the event by saying that they had decided not to invite the National Front candidate. Before he could finish his sentence, however, four men jumped out from the back of the crowds holding placards with 'Vote National Front' on them. They began shouting at the vicar and I swallowed hard as I thought back to the thugs who had chased me through the school grounds that time I skipped mosque when I was a kid. I may have run away from you then, I thought, but not any more.

The audience looked shocked, scared and concerned for the vicar as he tried to calm them down. I looked over at the other candidates, who all seemed to have retreated from the protest – most of them were looking down at their paperwork or writing notes. I looked across at the UKIP chap and he was laughing!

I admired the vicar for standing his ground, fearless. I kept my eye on their step as they got closer to him, ready to get up and put myself in between the two sides if things got physical. Thankfully, the police turned up within minutes and escorted them out – but they weren't leaving quietly.

Fifteen minutes later, the church was quiet again.

The vicar decided we should have another prayer and asked us to join him. I closed my eyes and my mind flashed back to all the canvassing dramas I had experienced. There was the man who almost punched me as he blamed 'my party' for the death of his brother, who had committed suicide because of his debts. The one who spat a cheese and pickle sandwich in my face as he told me he would rather vote for the National Front than for the Tories. The couple in the estate who set their dog on me when I got tired of people cutting me off mid-sentence and carried on talking over them. (The dog did the trick and since then I have never canvassed in an estate on my own again.)

The most productive door-knocking experience I'd had was a with a bloke who had vowed he would never vote for the Tories because they were all 'posh boys who don't understand how the other half lives'. 'I do,' I replied. 'I'm working class, and have experienced poverty, but I broke the cycle because this country gave me the opportunities.' It was the first time I saw change in someone's eyes, like they'd just cleaned their glasses and could see me properly now. It was the longest I'd stood at a doorstep and had a heart-to-heart with someone.

The prayer ended and finally the hustings began. As we were sat in alphabetical order, I was first up to give my opening statement. One of the first things I said was that my background was not political, but was varied, and I mentioned the fact that I had experiences with running a business, being in the British Army and being a governor at a special needs' school. I noticed a few eyebrows rise when I mentioned the army. I also told them I was born and bred in the area, came from an impoverished background and understood the local people and communities. I have come with fresh ideas, I said, and have ample energy to work together and build this town into one of the best in Britain.

Then it was on to the questions. Our answers were limited to one minute, after which a red flag would come out from one of the pillars at the back to tell us to stop. That was when I realised that my answers were too long; that the best parts were being cut off by the flag.

The first question was about poverty and how we would resolve the problem. Thankfully, they started with someone else this time, and we weren't going in alphabetical order for each question. It was good to hear other people's views on the matter, since what they said would spark other points that I could add to my answer. Some of the candidates talked about food banks; others talked about poverty in Britain.

I had collated some stats for these questions, and told the audience that 27 per cent of children in Rochdale live in poverty. I scanned the audience and noted that

I had caught a few of them off guard, perhaps because I was the only candidate who had localised the answer and, even though I didn't live in the area, I knew about Rochdale.

The next question was on the environment. I could tell by the looks on the candidates' faces that they didn't have much info at hand on this. I have to admit, I wasn't very well clued-up on it either, which is why I had extracted Budget figures on investing £200 million to make cycling safer, £500 million to ensure every car is zero-emission by 2050 and building new flood defences to protect 300,000 homes. None of the others could challenge my figures as they hadn't got any of their own. My opening remark was about the wind farms in Rochdale, which I now realised they all hated, but it at least made them engage with me.

A question was raised from the audience about Islamophobia and hate crimes in Rochdale. There were a few answers from the other candidates before my turn, some of whom said that there wasn't a problem and that we lived in a cohesive community. In my opening statement I said that there obviously was a problem, otherwise the question would not have been raised. I also added, which I do strongly believe, that the media has a lot to do with it, and that we needed to challenge the way the media puts out its news.

The final question was based on the NHS and health-care. This was the most complicated for me as, to be honest, all the party policies for the NHS seemed to blur into one another and nothing rang true. If I just regurgitate facts and figures like the others, I thought, nobody will remember me – as it was the last question and I was the last on the panel to answer, I needed to make an impact.

I decided to speak from the heart. I started by saying that I had seen many political parties go into government with different strategies for sorting out the NHS, but for some reason it was not working. I told the audience about my background in project management, and about the many times that clients had asked for the job to be finished earlier. This was never possible because each project has a fixed timeline and a process that can't be shortened, no matter how much money or what resources are thrown at it.

'This is exactly what we are doing with the NHS,' I continued. 'We are trying to fix the problems within a term of government, which is not working. We need to take the NHS out of politics and give it a ten-year plan. Regardless of what party gets in, we continue to work on the project independently to ensure a robust system that's good for the people, rather than a political party.'

The heads began to nod in the audience, and then the red flag was up. I managed to squeeze in my last sentence: 'The next best thing is to give another term to the Conservative Party so they can finish the job.'

The applause was amazing, and I knew it wasn't because I was suggesting that we give the Conservative Party another term, but because I said we should take the NHS out of politics. Afterwards I had Labour voters coming up to me to tell me that, though they would never vote for me because I was Tory, they thought I talked a lot of sense about the NHS. I stayed for a while longer, mingling with the locals, then headed out of the church.

The journey back to London that evening was tiring, and I was emotionally drained from all the adrenalin of the hustings. To my surprise, one of the imams from the earlier meeting had invited me to another hustings. It was scheduled for a week's time and amongst those in attendance would be 'influential Muslims, community leaders, businessmen and women's groups'. It was to be hosted by the Muslim engagement and development association.

As I entered the community hall on the night of the event, the first thing I noticed was that the room was about 95 per cent Muslim, and around two-thirds of the people were under thirty years old. I was soon approached a couple of young Muslim men who wanted to discuss my party policies, but they refused to shake my hand 'as it *wasn't Islamic*'.

As we took our seats I noted that UKIP had not been

invited for some reason. So it was just four of us: myself, candidates for Labour and Lib Dem and an independent candidate who had broken away from Labour.

I sat next to Simon Danczuk, who had a copy of the National Front leaflet with him. I did a double take when I saw the front cover: a picture of me, along with a few other Asian faces, with the slogan: 'Don't Waste Your Vote'. Surely, I thought, this can't be allowed!

Not surprisingly, the first question put to the candidates was about Islamophobia. The Lib Dem candidate stood up and started his response by saying: '*As-salamu alaykum* … It's the only Urdu I know.'

I laughed to myself. '*As-salamu alaykum*' was Arabic, not Urdu.

Later, questions were thrown at us from the audience. The sex-grooming scandal was first on the agenda, again unsurprisingly. Most of the questions were directed at Simon, but then one man stood up and accused him of publicly linking the rape of white girls with Pakistani men. He of course defended himself. People's expressions started to turn to anger as they accused Simon of stirring up racism within Rochdale's Muslim community as a result of comments he had made to the media. How appalling, I thought, nothing could be further from the truth.

'You should have been protecting us! … Why are you sat there laughing?' The shouting went on.

I sat back and listened. The commentator tried to steer the audience away to another, more national question, but the audience kept coming back to this same issue. It was how they were being perceived, every minute, every hour, every day in Rochdale that mattered most right now.

I'd thought that life with the SAS would be rough, but I was quickly learning that the world of politics could be rough too, especially when racial issues came to the fore, as they were clearly doing here. There's no doubt that my SAS training toughened me up mentally as well as physically, and made me ready to fight my corner. I can only imagine the kind of horrendous pressures the leaders of the major parties have to contend with.

Whatever the results in Rochdale and in the election generally, as I look to the future I realise what an invaluable grounding my experiences here have given me if I am to pursue a career in politics, as I most certainly intend to do.

I'd chosen a tough seat to fight and a tough area to fight in, but I don't regret that for a moment, and I'm proud to have had the opportunity to fight for the issues I believe in.

For me, this was just a beginning.

ACKNOWLEDGEMENTS

I AM INDEBTED to my agent David Grossman, without whom this book would not have been possible.

My thanks go to all my close friends whose enthusiasm and encouragement made writing this book a rewarding experience.

Finally, a special thanks to the army, the recruits, my trainers, Mike 22 SAS (my mentor in the army) and my colonel.